JOB'S WAY THROUGH PAIN

JOB'S WAY THROUGH PAIN

Karma, Clichés and Questions

Paul Hedley Jones

WIPF & STOCK · Eugene, Oregon

Wipf and Stock Publishers
199 W 8th Ave, Suite 3
Eugene, OR 97401

Job's Way Through Pain
Karma, Clichés and Questions
By Jones, Paul Hedley
Copyright © 2014 by Jones, Paul Hedley All rights reserved.
Softcover ISBN-13: 979-8-3852-5966-3
Hardcover ISBN-13: 979-8-3852-5967-0
eBook ISBN-13: 979-8-3852-5968-7
Publication date 7/29/2025
Previously published by Paternoster, 2014

This edition is a scanned facsimile of the original edition published in 2014.

For Elja, Kaylah and Solomon

Contents

Foreword (Richard S. Briggs)	ix
Acknowledgements	xi
Outline of the Book of Job	xiv

1. SETTING THE SCENE
A Way Through Pain	1
Explaining Experience	9
Karma, Clichés and Questions	15

2. KARMA
Karma in Kids	20
Blessings to Curses	24
Covered in Badness	30

3. CLICHÉS
Suffering, Silence, Sin	34
One Size Fits All?	39
A Web of Wisdom	41

4. QUESTIONS
Are Questions the Answer?	48
Wrestling with God: Rounds 1, 2 and 3	51
Dust and Ashes	57

5. CONVERSATION
Goats and Asses	63
A Change of Mind	67
Right Speech	71

6. THE GOSPEL OF JOB
Newfound Freedom   76
Pain + Prayer   79
From Karma to Grace   83

Bibliography   90
Endnotes   93

Foreword

Paul Jones knows that our best Bible reading does not distinguish between the academic and the practical, or the theological over against the spiritual, or the theoretical in contrast to the applied. Instead it engages all of our hearts and souls and minds and bodies in the profound task of wrestling with Scripture, and with the God of Jewish and Christian faith in and through Scripture.

In the book of Job he finds rich material for reflecting on all these aspects of the reading of a scriptural text. There are deep resources here for reflecting on how we might live, and how we might understand our lives, in the face of a God who is both loving and demanding; who seems both to invite us in and yet at the same time keep us at bay; as we try to understand the ways of God in our world and in our lives.

There are three particular reasons why I want to commend Paul's book. First, for the way it models that integrated task of taking Scripture seriously and spiritually. On one page you may find him writing movingly about lived experiences of pain and suffering, while on the next he may be offering insights into Hebrew vocabulary in pursuit of the best ways of reading a difficult verse. These belong together, especially with a text as challenging as the book of Job, but it is not so often that one sees them actually brought together as they are here.

Secondly, for its willingness to recognize the complex mixtures of passion and frustration which animate all the book's main characters: their insights and misunderstandings; their moments of pride and their moments of humility. Paul offers thought-provoking ways of reading such verses as God's words to Job's friends in chapter 42: 'you have not spoken of me what is right, as my servant Job has done' (42.8), ways which seek to do justice to our experience of reading this book of dramatic dialogues. How is Job right? And is he always right? And are the friends really always wrong? Isn't some of their theology fairly standard Old Testament theology? The book of Job consistently probes our expectations and pre-understandings on such matters, and Paul does that for us too as we read Job with him.

And thirdly, perhaps his most striking suggestion: the claim that the book of Job models the difference between talking *about* God and talking *to* God. Paul's book does that too. Of course this account is not the final word on the book of Job—who would expect there to be a final word on Job?—but it is a word that propels us back to take up once more our own conversations with God, as we too attempt to discern God's ways.

It is my pleasure to invite readers to join in that conversation; to seek the new insights and perspectives which Paul argues that Job himself is experiencing by the end of the book. I'm sure that in reading *Job's Way Through Pain* you won't find yourself ending up blessed with 14,000 sheep, 6,000 camels, or 1,000 oxen and donkeys, but in our own ways, as readers, the blessing of ongoing engagement with God—in good times and bad—awaits. Read on . . .

Richard S. Briggs
St. John's College
Durham University

Acknowledgements

The journey that led to the writing of this book began in July 2000, when I took a Summer School course at Regent College entitled 'Contending with the Silence of Heaven: A Reading of the Book of Job'. As a group of us met for class one Monday afternoon, Dr David Diewert introduced himself (as Dave) and proceeded to explain why we would not be taking the class within the walls of Regent College itself. It seemed inappropriate, he said, for us to discuss Job's intense suffering from the comfort of a cosy classroom with a coffee in one hand and a pen in the other. Dave didn't want human suffering to become an abstract theological problem for us to 'solve', nor did he want members of the class only to think about suffering from within the confines of their own experiences. And so, for the next two weeks we met in Vancouver's Downtown Eastside, an area well known since the 1980s for its drug and sex trades, criminal activity and extreme poverty. Dave organized for us to meet in a building at the intersection of Main and East Hastings, right at the heart of things, where the realities of poverty, prostitution and drugs are unavoidable.

Each day, the bus journey to class took us into unfamiliar territory. I was regularly offered drugs by people passing on the street and confronted with the deep turmoil of that neighbourhood. I remember watching one woman at the bus stop after class as she juggled a lighter, a loaded teaspoon and a syringe in fumbling but experienced hands. Many such images have stayed with me to this day. Now and then, our class was visited by members of the local community who shared their perceptions of God and the church—and they didn't hold back. On those days, I guess we felt a little like Job's friends, sitting on the ash heap and listening in stunned silence. On other occasions we took to the streets, warily taking in the sights, sounds and smells of the neighbourhood. I dare say most of us who took that course found ourselves immersed in two unfamiliar cultures over the summer: Vancouver's Downtown Eastside and the Ancient Near East. Dave's teaching was (typically) academically rigorous, and much of what I learned from that course has in some way or other informed the contents of this book. A short time after graduating, I discovered that Dave had left his full-time academic post at Regent to live in solidarity with the poor in his community. He continues to be a living testament to the theology he imparted to his students.

Only a year after returning to Australia, much of what I had learned about Job was consolidated in my own experience when my life, which had not previously met with many obstacles, hit a wall head-on. It was God's near-tangible presence and a couple of faithful friends that got me through that period. (Nathan Nettleton and Garry Deverell, I remain indebted and grateful to you both.)

More recently, the past two years have been spent in the northeast of England, in the beautiful city of Durham, which I have loved ever since we first came to visit. It has been a privilege to be part of the academic community in the theology department here as well as the slightly less formal group of PhD students who study (and eat noodles together every Friday) at 37a on the Bailey, right next door to the oldest cathedral in England. Whenever the cathedral and castle catch my eye (and they are hard to overlook), I am reminded of how blessed I am to be living and working in this remarkable place.

I am grateful to good friends in Durham who have devoted hours to proofreading drafts amidst busy schedules. In particular, I wish to thank Richard Briggs, Andy Byers, Wes Hill, Chris Juby and Orrey MacFarland, not just for helpful feedback on this project, but for their much-valued friendships. Once again, I am grateful to my editor Mike Parsons for his encouragement and faith in me, and I would like to express my deepest thanks to Jamie Coyle, Roslyn Jones and Wes Hill for sharing their painful, personal experiences with such honesty in the opening chapter. I especially thank my wife Anakatrina for giving me extra hours each week to work on a book that has nothing to do with my dissertation (and proofreading multiple versions of it!) and for being such a steadying presence in my life. Finally, I thank my heavenly Father for granting me resilience and grace. For when I am weak, then I am strong.

Paul Hedley Jones
October 2013

Outline of the Book of Job

1–2 Prologue
3   Job Curses His Birthday

4–14 **First Speech Cycle**
    4–5   Eliphaz
    6–7   Job
    8   Bildad
    9–10   Job
    11   Zophar
    12–14   Job

15–21 **Second Speech Cycle**
    15   Eliphaz
    16–17   Job
    18   Bildad
    19   Job
    20   Zophar
    21   Job

22–27 **Third Speech Cycle**
    22   Eliphaz
    23–24   Job
    25   Bildad
    26–27.12 Job
    27.13–23 Job (speaking for Zophar?)

28   Poem about Wisdom

29–31 Job's Final Speech

32–37 Elihu

38–41 Yahweh's Response

42   Epilogue

1

Setting the Scene

> *Life is pain, highness! Anybody that says different is selling something.*
> ~ WILLIAM GOLDMAN, The Princess Bride

A Way Through Pain

Pain, in its various shapes and shades, is an inevitable part of life, as Westley declares so memorably in *The Princess Bride*.[1] Equally certain is the fact that there are no easy answers to the problem of human suffering, and as you well know, anyone offering a quick-fix solution is probably up to no good.

The title of this book may give the impression that every painful experience gets left behind at some point, like a dark tunnel that disappears into the past once you manage to get through it. On the contrary, many wounds last a lifetime, and sometimes all we can do is try to come to terms with the hurt and then learn to wear the scars for the rest of our lives. In the opening lines of a memoir I read recently, the author describes the moment when her husband suffered a fatal coronary attack: *'Life changes in the instant. You sit down to dinner and life as you know it ends.'*[2] Such painful experiences (whether physical, emotional or psychological) paralyse us where we stand and steal our hope away, but they should not immobilize us forever. Even if we continue to be *in* pain for a very long time, it is important to keep moving *through* pain and to resist becoming stagnant.

To be clear from the outset, this book intends neither to eliminate your pain nor to enable you to ignore it. It has been written for those who, having experienced loss, trauma, grief or injustice, find themselves reaching for a hand in the hope of finding their feet again. My hope is that a better understanding of Job's way through pain will prove helpful for sufferers seeking to find their way forward and Godward. But before we are introduced to Job, let us begin where every such journey begins: with real-life experiences of suffering.

I have asked some friends if they would be willing to share something of their own hurts in this opening chapter, since many of the questions that grip us so powerfully are born of such events. Each of them, as you will see, is seeking to find a way through pain in order that life might go on, even when there is little or no hope that things will ever again be as they once were. I am deeply grateful to Jamie, Roslyn and Wesley for their willingness to write so openly in this context.

Jamie Coyle (Brisbane, Australia)

As a 5-year-old boy, one of the best things about a weekend was that Dad was around for forty-eight hours straight. Dad represented a heap of fun: playing cricket in the backyard; massive wrestles when I jumped on him in the mornings; getting him to build me ramps for my BMX; crazy, made-up stories that sent my imagination buzzing; and following him around doing big boy stuff.

The best time for this was when our house was being built in Melbourne and we moved to Coldstream, a small town in the Yarra Valley known for its vineyards. My grandparents ran a Brussels sprout farm out there. Not only did this mean more crazy adventures over weekends, chasing cows, making cubbies in gigantic oak trees, having mud fights when it rained (and it rained *a lot*), but I also got to mow the lawns with my dad on the ride-on lawnmower every Saturday. Dad would put me between himself and the steering wheel and off we would go. Every now and then he would let me steer the mower, which made me feel like king of the world.

One particular Saturday, Dad and I went to mow the lawns, but instead of putting me on his lap like we did most weeks he put me on the front of the mower where there were some handles that I could hold. I was alright with this because it felt like I was riding the mower like a skateboard and I had the front seat so I could see what we were just about to cut down. But as we were mowing my dad turned right, and because I wasn't holding on well enough, I fell to the left and my left arm went completely underneath the lawnmower.

There isn't a lot that I remember after this point except pulling my arm out and seeing blood and mess. I remember that my mum ran out and wrapped my arm in a purple towel, her picking me up and her holding me tightly as she and I climbed into the back of the green Toyota Corolla, which Dad drove to the nearest hospital as fast as that 2.0 litre engine could handle. And as I slipped into shock I remember seeing the purple towel turn red.

For the next seven years, from the age of 5 to 12, the doctors tried to rebuild my left hand. So much damage had been done by the blades of that lawnmower. It had shattered a lot of bone and taken much muscle, which was hard to replace.

When I think back over this season of being in and out of hospitals, the thing I found hardest was that when the time came for my mum to leave the hospital to go be with my sisters, I would be left alone. When I was scared in the night and I called out, it wasn't Mum that would come; it would be a nurse. When I cried, Mum wasn't there to hold me; it was a stranger.

In the years after my accident, another thing I found difficult was so desperately wanting to ride my BMX like all my mates. I'd watch them go over jumps and push themselves to crazy limits (as far as a 7-year-old could push) and I wished I could join in. But I found it hard to go over jumps as my left hand couldn't hold tight enough to the grip.

When I hit high school and the operations and hospital visits had all but come to an end, the realization that I was different hit me suddenly when other 12-year-old kids began to tease me about the weirdness of my hand. 'Four Fingers' was a popular nickname. Also, the movie *Nightmare on Elm Street* was in high circulation, so people would call me Freddy Krueger, because he had messed-up hands. Initially I was surprised and didn't think much of it, but after a period of time of people not wanting to hang out with me and having no real friends throughout the whole of Year 7, I desperately wanted to be 'normal'.

This motivated me to pursue whatever it would take to be liked. I did a heap of really dumb stuff in school in order to get people to like me or, at the very least, pay attention to me. When I hit Year 10, I took up surfing. I met some guys who would take me nearly every weekend, and over the course of two years I became decent at the sport. I also realized that people's attitudes changed towards me. My mates respected me because I surfed well, and the girls began to pay attention too. So I threw myself into the sport more and embraced everything that came with the surf culture.

But what I was really doing was just trying to push the pain away, push away how I really felt about myself and not deal with it. I would ignore my hand. I would try never to look at it and would put it in my pocket in public. I would shy away from using it, but still be confronted by it in the mirror.

I can't remember feeling angry at God for what happened. I don't think I blamed him for the accident, nor did I hold my dad responsible for it. But the questions that it raised were questions of identity and usefulness. I would wonder, 'How can someone like me, with a hand like this, be of use?' I would think, 'If I'm not normal, what am I?' I would fear failure and hesitate in making decisions because I didn't want to get that sinking feeling I got when I saw my hand. I guess I wondered how on earth God could make anything good come out of this. Because it didn't feel good.

At the age of 20, I was at a Christian surfers' event and I had an encounter with Jesus during worship like I had never experienced before. He didn't just touch my heart but he sowed a deep belief that he wanted to restore me and show me that he values me, he delights over me, and he calls me his own.

This took a while to really set in, but I began making a choice to not hide my hand and pretend it didn't exist. Instead of covering it up, I began talking about my hand and letting people see the real Jamie. I started by choosing not to leave it in my pocket at parties, at work and at church. When people asked, I would tell them my story and the story of Jesus reshaping me. And to my surprise, it impacted people. Things snowballed from there. I'm now in a band called Selahphonic and we tour many places in the world using music and film to communicate the great news of Jesus. My left hand is a big part of that message.

While I was picking up my 9-year-old son from school the other day, his friends gathered around to look at my hand and ask the harsh, blunt questions only kids know how to ask. As we walked home, he grabbed hold of my hand, looked up at me and said, 'Dad, I wouldn't want you any other way. I love that you are different.'

Roslyn Jones (Melbourne, Australia)

When we lost our little Solomon, born prematurely after a harrowing four days of desperate hope mixed with terrifying fear, I felt like I'd been washed up on the shore. I'd been cruising on what seemed like gentle currents, moving cautiously along in my pregnancy. Things were going well, he was following the growth charts, I had entered the 'home straight', and then suddenly out of the blue I was caught up by a freak wave and dumped on a sandbar, tumbled about, the life literally sucked out of me, barely knowing which way was up.

It felt as if a core part of me had been ripped away and I was left with a gaping void that resounded with aches and groans. Only those who have experienced grief that intense would know what I mean by those aches and groans. I was not prepared for the physical and emotional trauma of being separated from that little life growing within me, of holding his lifeless, peaceful body in my arms, seeing his tiny features perfectly formed and knowing it was the first and last time I would hold him close, of leaving the maternity hospital with empty arms, leaving my baby boy behind me, with just my bag and a few belongings, passing visitors in the lift bearing flowers and presents for someone else's 'bundle of joy'. How can I ever forget that stabbing pain, sorrow and anguish? I felt, and still do, a strong longing for eternity – because a part of me was there now and had connected me to it in a very real, flesh-and-blood way. I wanted to know more about what lay beyond this life and where my son had gone.

I remember in those early days, weeks and months, trying to make some sense of it all – what can we trust God for? I mean, what really is guaranteed? Is anything safe? I believed in miracles, I believed that God answers prayer, I believed his promises of protection, I believed he wants the best for us, but how could *this* be his best? I believed that he does want to 'bless', but my notions of blessing were being torn apart. What now? If he can allow a long-prayed-for, innocent, vulnerable baby to be taken, what else might I have to lose? I'd already had two miscarriages (both before and after my daughter was born) and I had trusted intercessors praying for this pregnancy. Surely God would have mercy on me and allow this pregnancy to go to full term? But it was not to be. Nor would it for another two pregnancies after Solomon, just more crushing heartbreak.

So what does it mean to 'have faith'? It's all very well to spout the head knowledge, but another thing completely to hold to that conviction when something so dear and priceless is taken. Each day, the sadness hovers around like a shadow and I just want to cry out to heaven, 'Solomon, I miss you! Come back. I want to see your little face; I want to know what your voice sounds like. Your sister misses you and often says she wishes you were here.' Where is God then to neatly patch it all up and make things better, and restore what was lost? How do you learn to live with the sense of incompleteness and yearning for what is missing? What do you do if simply 'having another one' (as some people thoughtlessly suggest, as if one life can replace another) doesn't happen or results in more loss? I have no clear answers, but perhaps I'm gradually coming to identify, even if only intermittently and somewhat reluctantly, with a quote previously unknown to me from a letter written by C.S. Lewis: 'We're not necessarily doubting that God will do the best for us; we are wondering how painful the best will turn out to be.' Learning to live with that tension between sadness and hope is a daily struggle.

In my reflections and readings following multiple losses, I have come to appreciate the significance of having an 'Ebenezer' in my life (1 Samuel 7–12); a 'stone of help' that signifies God's help and guidance in my life so far and his spiritual work through what I've experienced. Through God's grace I have made it to today. Without it, I would not be where I am. And as Samuel built his Ebenezer to God, so I had my own 'Ebenezer' made, a remembrance ring to remind me to thank and praise God, even in the hardest of times when it's most difficult to trust him. This ring—and I look at it often—calls me to remember God's promises to me of mercy, restoration, healing and redemption, of beauty, hope, new directions, visions and dreams. It is to bear witness to God's living and active presence in my life, despite what I may feel, and his promises to help me in times of deepest trouble and need. I had the ring designed to also represent all five heavenly darlings waiting to meet me, so I can hold them close to me and know that one day I will hold my treasured children, one day when the sting of death is gone and the reality of eternal life shines bright. It is something concrete to bring some certainty to what I hope for, and it is a truly beautiful ring to me for so many reasons.

Many times I have felt confused and questioned whether I can really trust God. I've been angry at God for allowing it to happen and distressed by the insensitivities and seeming indifference of others who couldn't understand. But deep down I've known the only way forward is to run to God and not away. As long as I keep going towards him, even when I don't understand his ways or he seems so silent, I will find life. Trying to live away from God will only turn my pain into chaos and despair. Nor can I bear the thought of Solomon's life being wasted or his death being in vain. I need something good to come from it; otherwise hope drains away. It's not the 'good' I wanted or that anyone would wish for, but I cling to the promise that another 'good' will come from it, something that previously I could only have dreamed about. It's the crushing of incense that releases fragrance, the pressing of olives that allows the oil of anointing to flow—I have to believe and trust that God will bring a healing balm from this sorrow and that it will yield a harvest of righteousness in his time.

Some days when I visit the 'butterfly lawn' (an area of the cemetery dedicated to babies and toddlers) and place fresh flowers on Solomon's grave, I wander over to the other little sites and read the plaques, the cards and decorations. No single place in the cemetery has as much grief poured out in it as this section, and no sites are as collectively well-tended and adorned as these. And then I wonder what I'm doing here! This is not how I envisaged loving my son. Yet I have to love him somehow even though he is not here physically. Finding ways to express that love, when he is not here to receive or return it, is an ongoing quest for me. It's also been a very lonely journey, for who wants to accompany someone to a child's grave?

Wesley Hill (Ambridge, Philadelphia)[3]
How do you deal with an ongoing ache, one that won't go away, no matter how much you pray? That question has haunted me like a recurrent, unpleasant chill, for the duration of my Christian life. From a young age, growing up in church, I learned how to tell stories of aches that aren't ongoing. I mastered the art of the 'I once was blind but now I see' sort of testimony, in which a painful past gives way to a peaceful present. I learned how to speak of 'victory' and 'transformation' and 'change'. What I didn't learn as well—and what still rattles me now—is how to tell a story of persistent pain, the sort of pain that you expect to be around a year from now, and the year after that, and most likely the year after that . . . with no relief in sight.

As I was making the transition from childhood to adolescence and deepening my involvement at the church of my upbringing, I was also waking up to the unwelcome realization that I liked guys, not girls. I mouthed the words silently in my bed at night: homosexual, homosexuality. At the time when my guy friends were beginning to notice girls, I was beginning to notice *them*. Their changing bodies fascinated me, and whenever I had a crush, it was on one of my friends, rather than on someone 'normal'— namely, a girl.

My prayer, throughout the remainder of my adolescence and on into my college years, was that God would take away these desires. I dreamed of some dramatic but secret cure, one that would allow me the relief of never having to tell anyone else about my attractions, and then to experience the joy of heterosexual marriage. I pictured arriving as a freshman at my college campus, meeting 'the right girl', and having my homosexuality melt away, like a fog whose disappearance you barely notice, so quick and subtle is its vanquishing in the midmorning heat.

But that didn't happen. I prayed and prayed and met with pastors and counsellors, finally confiding in a select few. To no avail. My sexual orientation, if anything, solidified.

Perhaps that meant I should revisit what I'd been taught growing up—that the Bible and Christian tradition were unanimous in defining marriage as the union of one man and one woman. Could I have been wrong about that? Might there be room for a Christian to affirm gay marriage?

Gradually, I came to the realization that I was vacillating between two escape routes: either I wanted my sexual orientation to change from homosexual to heterosexual, so that I could marry a woman and not have to live in the tension of unfulfilled desire any more, or else I wanted my Christian convictions to change from 'traditional' to 'revisionist', so that I could marry a man and not have to live in the tension of unfulfilled desire any more. But it finally dawned on me that perhaps God was, at least at the moment, less interested in offering me an escape route and more interested in my present life-in-tension itself.

The Catholic theologian Josef Pieper talks about the Christian virtue of hope as perched precariously between two pitfalls. On the one hand, hope teeters over the brink of presumption. Presumption is the belief that you've already arrived, so there's no need for hope. (As St Paul says, hope that is already seen ceases to be hope at all.[4]) On the other hand, hope teeters over the opposite brink of despair. Despair is the belief that you'll never arrive, and there's no need for hope in that place either, since one who is certain that there is no destination has given up hope. Avoiding both these abysses, Pieper says, hope is the characteristic virtue of wayfarers—those who know that they have not already arrived, who refuse nevertheless to give up the journey as a lost cause, but continue to put one foot ahead of the other, choosing to embrace their pilgrim status.

When I speak about ongoing pain on the journey, I'm talking about the pain of the wayfarer. Most of the time I wish I weren't on the road. I'd rather be at home and at rest, either in a straight or gay marriage. I'd rather not be lonely, as I am much of the time. I'd rather not be gay and celibate, on this paradoxical edge of neither being rescued from my homosexual orientation nor rescued from the state of being single. There are nights when an empty bed is the saddest thing I can think of.

But what I am learning to see is that my kind of situation, of finding oneself poised on the edge, struggling to maintain balance and not fall off on either side, is perhaps not necessarily a sign of being in the wrong. Perhaps the pain that I and others in my shoes experience simply means that we're 'on the way' and that God, mysteriously, silently, is with us.

In one of his prison letters, Dietrich Bonhoeffer writes, 'My thoughts and feelings seem to be getting more and more like those of the Old Testament, and in recent months I have been reading the Old Testament much more than the New... In my opinion it is not Christian to want to take our thoughts and feelings too quickly and too directly from the New Testament.'[5] In context, what Bonhoeffer seems to be saying that is we must feel ourselves to be waiting for the promised hope, yearning to see God's face, before we can truly grasp what the embodiment of that hope might mean for us.

I think I know what he means. I feel that tension of being on the way, of not having arrived. No victory or transformation is in sight. With Job, I am waiting for the day when my Redeemer will at last stand upon the earth (Job 19.25), and I'll be there at his side. But that day hasn't come yet.

Explaining Experience

A fundamental aspect of being human is the need to explain our experiences, and this is certainly true for Jamie, Roslyn and Wes. *How can someone like me, with a hand like this, be of use? If he can allow a long-prayed-for, innocent, vulnerable baby to be taken, what else might I have to lose? How do you deal with an ongoing ache, one that won't go away, no matter how much you pray?* As well as questions specific to our circumstances, painful experiences raise more general questions, too. Does God cause bad things to happen, or does he merely allow them to happen? In either case, why doesn't God prevent bad things from happening to good people? And how are we to understand it when such things do happen? Are they part of an overarching, divine plan (i.e. God's best for us)? Should they be understood as punishment? Or is there some other explanation?

The book of Job tells the story of one man's desperate struggle to understand his own suffering, and when the book is considered as a whole, the proportion of space devoted to explaining Job's experiences says a great deal. After the opening chapters, which recount a series of injustices that strike hard upon Job's settled existence, the next forty chapters report the efforts of Job and his friends to explain what has happened. That's right: forty chapters! At the end, a brief epilogue (less than a chapter) reveals how Job has been changed by the whole saga. But the fact that such a bulky proportion of the book is given to explaining Job's experience cannot go unnoticed.

When life's events do not match up with our beliefs, some form of explanation is required. Either our beliefs are wrong-headed or our experiences are not what they seem. Something must give. If, for instance, you firmly believe that ghosts are not real, but you wake one night to find one standing at the foot of your bed, then you will need to either modify your beliefs about ghosts or find a way to explain what has happened. (Is someone playing a trick on you? Are you fully awake? Did you recognize the ghost as someone who recently passed away?) It is not a question of being curious or intelligent so much as a matter of being human. We want the stuff of life to be coherent. Our experiences need to make sense.

In Job's case, his suffering leads him to reconsider how the world operates. At the beginning of his story, as we shall see, Job believes that bad things happen to bad people and good things happen to good people. He is then thrown into a muddle when tragedy strikes, because Job is confident (for good reason) that he lives a morally good life. Two basic conclusions present themselves: (a) Job is not as good as he supposes (and his friends will try very hard to convince him of this), or (b) Job's assumptions about the world—that bad things only happen to those who deserve it—are misguided. Whatever conclusions Job ultimately reaches, the important thing for us to note from the outset is that Job cannot stay the same. Change is afoot.

I was reminded of the importance of the development in Job's character when I was on the phone recently with someone who has endured a great deal of pain and loss. As we were talking, she asked why Job is said to have great wealth and many children both at the beginning and at the conclusion of his story. She thought it strange (and rightly so) that the ending seems to indicate that nothing really changes, for as we intuitively know, stories go nowhere unless something changes. When the book of Job is read as a unified story, the question of what *happens* to Job becomes very important, for if he ends up right back where he started, then we may well ask, what is the point of it all? In chapter six, we will see that the biblical storytellers did not tack a simplistic 'happily ever after' ending onto Job's story in a rushed attempt to tie up loose ends. There's certainly more going on than that.

If we attempt to trace positive change in Job's character, however, one obvious problem presents itself: namely, how can someone who is introduced as 'a true man of integrity' *develop*? What more can be expected of someone who habitually fears God and turns away from evil? Moreover, throughout most of the book Job sits on a pile of ashes where he appears to do little other than talk and listen. How are we to measure the progress of a man who hardly *does* anything?

As it turns out, shifts in Job's character are manifested in what he says. The terms of the wager between God and the Accuser[6] set a spotlight not upon Job's actions but upon his words, so that readers are prompted to follow what is happening to Job by noting changes in his God-talk, i.e. the way he talks to and about God. The question of *right speech* pervades the entire book of Job. It is introduced in the prologue ('see if he doesn't curse you to your face!') in such a way that it stays in the minds of readers as they hear the speeches, and it is the key phrase in God's vindication of Job in the epilogue ('You have not spoken to me rightly, as my servant Job has').

This issue of right speech resonates powerfully in the lives of all those who are trying to understand their suffering in the context of life with God. It can feel rather tiresome to keep praying *to* a God who doesn't seem to respond, just as it is difficult to speak 'rightly' *about* a God who feels absent. Or, to put the matter more bluntly, what good is a God who does not prevent pain and rescue his creatures from injustice? When life treats us terribly, is such a God even worthy of right speech? And if we insist that he is, what constitutes right speech anyway? The book of Job frames such questions with a story in which Job suffers significant losses in order that his God-talk may be weighed and measured. Job's words reveal what is happening to him. But we are getting ahead of ourselves with talk of Job's character development. Let us turn to the opening chapters of the story itself.

> **THE ACCUSER**
>
> Most Bible translations call this member of the heavenly council 'Satan', bringing to mind a treacherous, horned, demonic character, perhaps even with pitchfork in hand. In this book, I refer to this character as 'the Accuser', so a word of explanation is perhaps in order. To put it briefly, we must do what we can to get the name 'Satan' out of our heads when reading Job 1–2. When the book of Job was written, the personification of evil known as 'the devil' was in the minds of neither writers nor readers. That is to say, this member of the heavenly council who challenges God in the Job story is not Satan with a capital S. To read the story that way is to project a New Testament understanding of the devil back onto a text written hundreds of years earlier. In the book of Job, *hasatan* is best thought of as a job description rather than a name.

The book of Job begins with five scenes that alternate back and forth between earth (left column below) and heaven (right column below). Reading Job, we have the heavenly realm opened to us. The way the story is presented thereby allows us to identify with Job's trials while at the same time remaining outside his situation enough to engage with the theological questions that are raised. We are not supposed to infer from Job's story that every human struggle is undergirded by tests and wagers in the heavenly realm. Certainly not! One recent commentary has helpfully put it in these terms:

> In a word, we are not given a literal description of how God or how heaven actually works. This depiction is for storytelling purposes only: to tell the reader in no uncertain terms that Job is innocent and that his suffering is not the result of any infraction of God's law ... the broader purpose is to create a story to illustrate that not all suffering is the result of someone's sin.[7]

The five opening scenes read as follows (all citations from the book of Job in this book are my own translation):

Scene one
1.1 Once there was a man in the land of Uz, and his name was Job. This was a true man of integrity; he feared God and turned away from badness.
1.2 And he brought into the world seven sons and three daughters.
1.3 He owned 7,000 sheep, 3,000 camels, 500 pairs of oxen, 500 donkeys, and also a huge number of servants. In fact, he was the most renowned person in the East.
1.4 Now his sons used to hold parties, each in his house in turn, and they would send invitations to their three sisters to eat and drink with them.
1.5 And when the days of feasting reached their completion, Job would dedicate them to God; he would get himself up early in the morning and offer up burnt offerings according to their number. For Job thought, 'Perhaps my children have sinned, and cursed God in their hearts.' This was Job's regular habit.

Scene two

1.6 One day the heavenly beings took their places before Yahweh, and the Accuser was also in their midst.
1.7 Yahweh asked the Accuser, 'Where have you been?' And the Accuser answered Yahweh, saying, 'I've been scouring the earth as I travel around in it.'
1.8 Yahweh asked the Accuser, 'Have you investigated my servant Job? For there is none on earth like him; he is truly a man of integrity, one who fears God and turns away from badness.'
1.9 'But does Job fear God for nothing?' the Accuser replied.
1.10 'Have you not hedged him in on all sides, together with his house and all that he owns? You bless every work of his hands, and his cattle inundate the land!
1.11 But now, stretch out your hand and afflict all that belongs to him, and see if he doesn't curse you to your face!'
1.12 Then Yahweh said to the Accuser, 'Look, all that belongs to him is in your hands. Just don't lay a finger on him.' And the Accuser left Yahweh's presence.

Scene three

1.13 One day, when his sons and daughters were eating, and drinking wine, in the home of their eldest brother,
1.14 a messenger came to Job and said, 'The oxen were ploughing and the donkeys were grazing nearby,
1.15 when the Sabeans attacked them and took them. The servants were all killed with the sword, but I have escaped—only me—in order to tell you.'
1.16 While that one was still speaking, another one came and said, 'Fire from God has fallen from the heavens and burnt up the flocks and servants; it has completely consumed them, but I have escaped—only me—in order to tell you.'
1.17 While that one was still speaking, another one came and said, 'The Chaldeans formed three

companies and raided the camels and took them. The servants were all killed with the sword, but I have escaped—only me—in order to tell you.'

1.18 While that one was still speaking, another one came and said, 'Your sons and daughters were eating and drinking wine in the house of their eldest brother, **1.19** and suddenly a mighty wind came out of the desert and buffeted the four corners of the house, and it fell upon the servants and killed them, but I have escaped—only me—in order to tell you.'

1.20 Job stood up, tore his robe and shaved his head. Then he fell to the ground and worshipped.

1.21 He said, 'I left my mother's womb naked, and I will die naked. Yahweh gives and Yahweh takes away. Blessed be the name of Yahweh!'

1.22 In all this, Job did not sin or blame God.

Scene four

2.1 One day the sons of the gods came and presented themselves before Yahweh, and the Accuser was also in their midst, to present himself before Yahweh.

2.2 Yahweh asked the Accuser, 'Where have you been?'

And the Accuser answered Yahweh, saying, 'I've been scouring the earth as I walk around in it.'

2.3 Then Yahweh asked the Accuser, 'Have you investigated my servant Job? For there is none on earth like him; he is truly a man of integrity, one who fears God and turns away from badness. And he still remains strong in his integrity, even though you urged me to destroy him—for nothing.'

2.4 'Skin for skin!' the Accuser replied. 'A man would give everything for the sake of his life!

2.5 So now, reach out your hand and afflict his flesh and bones, and see if he doesn't curse you to your face!'

2.6 Then Yahweh said to the Accuser, 'Look, he is in your hands. But preserve his life.'

2.7a So the Accuser departed from Yahweh's presence.

Scene five
2.7b And he inflicted Job with terrible ulcers, from the soles of his feet to the crown of his head.
2.8 Job took a broken piece of pottery in order to scrape himself with it, and he sat among the ashes.
2.9 But his wife said to him, 'Do you still remain strong in your integrity? Curse God and die!'
2.10 But he said to her, 'What you're saying is like the speech of one of the foolish women. If we accept good things from the hand of God, should we not also accept bad things?'
In all this, Job did not sin with his lips.
2.11 Now, when three of Job's friends heard about all this badness that had come upon him, they came, each from his place—Eliphaz the Temanite, Bildad the Shuhite, and Zophar the Naamathite. They arranged to meet together in order to come and show their sympathy and comfort him.
2.12 But when they lifted their eyes from afar, they did not even recognize him. So they lifted their voices and wailed. Each of them tore his robe, and they threw dust in the air over their heads.
2.13 And they sat with him on the ground for seven days and seven nights. But not a word was spoken to him, for they could see that his pain was excessive.

Karma, Clichés and Questions

Job's story is an ancient one (two to three thousand years old) about a formidable character who endured almost every kind of suffering imaginable—natural disasters, the loss of children, renunciation from his wife, a horrid skin disease, and exclusion from his community—all the while adamantly insisting before God and his friends that he was definitely *not* getting what he deserved. Job's relentless drive to understand his experience has led to the composition of hundreds, even thousands, of inspirational books, plays, sculptures, songs, poems and paintings over the past two millennia.[8] In this book, I am using the three-stage framework indicated in the book's subtitle to better understand how Job works out the tension between his beliefs and his experiences. This structure highlights the main options available to Job as he seeks to understand the cause and purpose of his suffering.

The ordering of these three stages, *from* karma *to* clichés *to* questions, is only broadly sequential, however. Quite often, the clichés presented by Job's friends throughout chapters 4–27 are simply reformulations of karma, to which Job continually responds by directing questions back at his friends or God. The chapters on karma and clichés therefore contain some overlap, since the clichés of the friends are saturated with a theology of just desserts. The chapter on karma deals with the *content* of the friends' theology, whereas the chapter on clichés focuses on the *form* of their speech; i.e. the dangers of reducing complex realities and truths to simple formulas. In contrast, Job's open-ended questions (chapter four) represent a shift away from certainty into the unknown. I will introduce each chapter here to give an overview of the book's contents.

The focus of chapter two is Job's initial conviction that people get what they deserve in life, a principle best known in common parlance as '**karma**'. (In the interests of readers who may be sensitive to the beliefs of Hinduism, Buddhism and Sikhism, I should clarify that I mean no disrespect by taking a term that has deep religious significance in certain circles and using it in a simpler fashion. I am merely using the word 'karma' as shorthand for the belief that one always reaps what one sows in life.) Unexpected tragedy in Job's life forces him to rethink his belief that God always enforces karma. It becomes suddenly and painfully apparent to him that one does not necessarily 'get' according to what one 'gives', that what 'goes around' does not always 'come around', that turning *towards* God and *away* from evil does not guarantee a life of health and wealth.

Chapter three highlights the inadequacy of **clichés**, which spill all too easily through the lips of Job's friends. Eliphaz, Bildad and Zophar respond to Job's suffering with a variety of religious platitudes, many of which can still be heard today from well-meaning friends. It is true that most clichés are clichés for good reason (i.e. they have some merit), but they are a completely inappropriate way of dealing with the incalculable depths of human suffering and grief. As his friends repeatedly reduce the complexities of life to bite-size solutions, Job finds himself increasingly dissatisfied—*frustrated* is a better word—with their clichés. Chapter three concludes by exploring how the Bible, as a 'web of wisdom', contains a range of testimonies about God, each of which deserves our full attention. Learning to hold different voices together is in some ways like learning to juggle, but it is well worth the effort.

In chapter four, we examine Job's bold **questions** as he presents his case before (and *against*) God. In basic terms, Job believes that he deserves a better hand than the one he has been dealt. We will see that Job speaks as though he were in a law court, and that he finds it increasingly difficult to directly address a God who does not appear to be paying much attention. Job's confrontational manner is alarming—e.g. 'Why have you made me your target?' in 7.20—and in his final speech Job goes so far as to accuse God of being a cosmic bully whose haphazard form of governance has led to Job's unmaking. He concludes his final speech with a demand that the Almighty answer for his ways.

Chapter five outlines the **conversation** that ensues as a consequence of the charges Job has brought against his Maker. God does not answer as we (or Job) might hope or expect; instead of offering a logical response to the problem of human pain, God chooses instead to talk about rainclouds and ostriches. When we look more closely, however, God does address the primary issues Job has raised, of order and entitlement. In turn, Job declares that his eyes have been opened and his mind changed (42.5–6), though in what precise ways we shall have to wait and see. In light of God's positive evaluation of Job's speech—and considering some of the accusations Job has levelled against him!—we will ask in what ways Job has spoken 'rightly' (42.7–8).

The final chapter draws out the **gospel** ('good news') in the book of Job by examining how the conversation between Job and God has a transformative effect on Job, indicated by numerous details in the closing verses of the story. Following Job's disillusionment with karma, his frustration with the clichéd wisdom of his friends, and his honest and aggressive questioning of God, the book's epilogue takes us beyond God-talk and permits us to observe what shifts also occur in Job's behaviour. The basic dynamic of Job's experience, a movement from karma to grace, is also identified in the life of the apostle Paul, and by way of conclusion a brief theology of suffering is offered in answer to the question, 'Why is pain necessary?'

Throughout this book, as you consider Job's story in light of your own, it is my hope that you will find the courage to question the security of karma, to push past hackneyed clichés (found as often within the church's walls as on bookshelves), and to fully engage God with your questions. If what you're looking for is a reasoned, logical explanation for why God permits evil and injustice to affect our lives, it may never come. Job certainly didn't get that kind of answer. But if, like Job, you are willing to face the Tempest with life's questions held out boldly before you, you will almost certainly emerge a different person once the storm has passed. And that may turn out to be a better answer than the one you were looking for.

Dig Deeper

- With which of the three testimonies on pages 2–9 do you most identify? Why?

- How have painful experiences in your life affected your understanding of God?

- Life experiences can lead to certain changs in a person's character. In what ways are you in control and/or not in control of this process?

- How do you respond when bad things intrude upon your life?

- How do you speak to and about God when you are experiencing pain or injustice?

2

Karma

> *For every action, there is an equal and opposite reaction.*
> ~ NEWTON'S THIRD LAW

Karma in Kids

Over the past twenty years, I've had the opportunity to work in a wide range of contexts, including factories, bookstores, schools and churches. In each of those environments, I encountered people who considered karma to be as dependable as the daily rising of the sun. When something fared well for someone, it was, naturally, because that person had earned it. Equally, when things took a turn for the worse, well, anyone could see they had it coming to them. This so-called 'law' of karma is so certain in some people's minds that when bad things happen, you will sometimes even hear them say things like, 'I must have done *something* to deserve this.' As we noted in chapter one, people naturally feel compelled to explain their experiences, and in many cases karma provides an easy answer. But where does this idea come from, that what we get in life must necessarily be what we deserve?

The Swiss developmental psychologist Jean Piaget discovered that most children establish the conviction very early in life that they inhabit a just world. Without needing to be taught about justice and retribution, children are intuitively aware that badness deserves punishment as surely as goodness deserves reward. (How often must parents respond to the objection, 'That's not fair!' from their kids!) Moreover, children tend to believe not only that certain consequences are deserved, but also that this fair world we live in has a way of ensuring that people get their just desserts. In one experiment Piaget conducted, children aged between 6 and 12 were told a series of three simple stories, one of which went like this:

> Once there were two children who were stealing apples in an orchard. Suddenly a policeman comes along and the two children run away. One of them is caught. The other, going home by a roundabout way, crosses a river on a rotten bridge and falls into the water.[1]

When questioned about these events, 86% of children aged 6 deduced that the act of theft was what caused the bridge to collapse. In other words, the second child would not have fallen into the river if he or she had not stolen the apples. These 6-year-olds expressed a belief in what Piaget called 'immanent justice', the idea that wrongdoing inevitably leads to punishment. Apparently, we become convinced very early in life that the world turns on a karmic axis.[3] It is interesting, however, that in Piaget's experiment, the responses of older children were less unanimous. Only 34% of 11- and 12-year-olds perceived the bridge's collapse as punishment for the stolen apples.

> **KARMA**
>
> Karma is the Sanskrit word for 'action', referring to a deed with certain consequences. (The relationship between cause and effect is a central concept within a number of Eastern religions.) The German sociologist Max Weber referred to karma as a kind of cultural doctrine in India. He wrote that 'karma doctrine transformed the world into a strictly rational, ethically-determined cosmos.'[2]
>
> In the Western world, too, karma is generally understood as a natural law that enforces justice, somehow built into the fabric of the universe; a kind of universal police officer who takes note of what we do and deals out consequences accordingly (although the image of a police officer is too personal). And while the law of karma—yes, it is sometimes referred to as a 'law'—cannot be scientifically measured like gravity or time, it is taken to be equally resolute, perhaps a kind of 'spiritual' or 'moral' law with serious repercussions. Since karma is considered to be both descriptive (telling us how things are) and prescriptive (instructing us how to behave), it has a powerful influence over the lives of those who believe in it.

As we grow up and begin to see for ourselves that life is not always fair, we are confronted with a basic choice: we can either question the certainty of karma or cling to the notion of deservedness all the more firmly. I suspect that many people prefer the latter option because they would like to believe that the world is managed by a trustworthy, universal police officer (whom some would call 'God'). But holding fast to karma in a world that does not always play by the rules can lead to a cold lack of empathy. As one recent study concludes, 'Many people believe the world is a just place, which leads them to blame the victims of tragedies for their misfortune.'[4] If the world has a way of ensuring that we are always treated fairly, do we only have ourselves to blame when trouble comes our way?

I remember struggling with this question as a teenager when my mother, who had faithfully served God as a missionary in Africa for twelve years, suddenly became the victim of an aggressive case of rheumatoid arthritis. As her body deteriorated over the twenty-four years that followed, she suffered not just physical pain but also the deeper losses of freedom and self-worth. By the time her struggle against the disease came to an end, she had steel joints in both knees, both hips and one shoulder, not to mention plastic knuckle replacements in both hands and the permanent removal of all the metacarpals in her toes. (She used to joke about her body being discovered in the future and mistaken for a bionic woman. 'How very ironic that would be!' she would say.) As time passed, I remember all the prayer meetings and healing sessions, some of them attended by our whole family. She remained so hopeful about each one and so confused afterwards as her tortured body continued to take turns for the worse. I simply couldn't understand it. I had heard healing stories at church and personally known people with amazing stories to tell of God's miraculous intervention in their lives. So why not my mother? After all, she had devoted so much of her life to missionary work and being heavily involved in the life of the church. She had even continued to teach religious education in the local primary school until she could no longer walk. It just wasn't fair. She deserved better.

Seeing my mother's health deteriorate forced me to think through this question of karma, the idea that what we get in life must necessarily be what we deserve. I searched for a way to understand her painful condition in relation to my belief in a loving, healing God. To settle for the notion that everything in life is fair (because God ensures it) implied that my mother somehow deserved her arthritis. The alternative—to question my assumptions about the place of suffering in a life of Christian faith—was a long and winding road, but I took it (and am still on it). Over time, I came to recognize that it is OK to ask tough questions of God, to express my anger about injustice before God, and even to tell him directly that I have no idea why he never healed my mum. Seeing her suffer for so many years shattered my belief that people always get what they deserve in this life. Or, from another point of view, it encouraged me to search for a more meaningful way of understanding God and injustice.

But where can we turn for answers? Church, after all, is one of the places where we are often taught as children—and adults, for that matter—that we can establish a kind of quid pro quo arrangement with God; honour God with your life and enjoy his blessings in return. (Some churches even proclaim quite emphatically that Christians should *always* be rich, healthy, happy and successful.) Does the Bible have anything helpful to say about the relationship between karma and Christianity, or does it just muddy the waters? Clearly, at least some parts of the Bible support the idea that God makes sure people get what they deserve:

> For the arms of the wicked shall be broken,
>   but the Lord upholds the righteous (Ps 37.17 NRSV).

> The perverse get what their ways deserve,
>   and the good, what their deeds deserve (Prov 14.14 NRSV).

Piaget sought to demonstrate that most children start life with a shared basic expectation: the world is just and we get what we give. But this is hardly a childish notion. The related idea that *all people have sinned and must therefore suffer* not only finds support in the so-called wisdom literature of the Old Testament (books like Proverbs); biblical scholars and ancient historians tell us that this insight was 'common in the whole of the ancient world',[5] and I probably don't need to inform you that the same belief prevails today in all circles of life. This makes Job's story all the more important for us, not just because Job is one of the Bible's wisdom books, but because at the beginning of his tale he shares our convictions about how the world ought to operate.

Blessings to Curses

The book of Job may seem long-winded, but the opening verses get straight down to business. In just a few lines, the narrator subtly raises the notion of deservedness by introducing Job with two basic observations: Job is morally upright (v. 1) and he is exceedingly wealthy (vv. 2–3).[6] What is *not* said is whether these two facts are related to one another. Is Job rich because he is righteous? Righteous because he is rich? What does Job himself think? Does he perceive a link between his vast wealth and his integrity? It would appear from the information provided that he does, for prior to the devastation that overcomes Job and his family, the narrative takes a moment to outline our protagonist's rather compulsive habit:

> Now his sons used to hold parties, each in his house in turn, and they would send invitations to their three sisters to eat and drink with them. And when the days of feasting reached their completion, Job would send for them and consecrate them; he would get himself up early in the morning and offer up burnt offerings according to the number of them all. For Job thought, 'Perhaps my children have sinned, and cursed God in their hearts.' This was Job's regular habit (Job 1.4–5).

Now, on one hand, we could see this as a positive portrayal of Job: his very first words express fatherly concern for the kinds of things his children might mutter when they are 'under the influence'. Job is presented as one who speaks (by praying) on behalf of others. But on the other hand, the logic of Job's behaviour implies that he holds a fairly mechanical view of God. He thinks, 'Perhaps my children have sinned,' and on that basis offers a sacrifice on their behalf. The rationale, at least in Job's mind, is straightforward: if Job is not dutiful in securing forgiveness for his children through burnt offerings, then something bad might befall them. Job's (trans)actions say a great deal about his beliefs: Sin and you will suffer; make amends and you will be OK—at least, until the next wild party. Blessings and curses are both real possibilities, but whatever decisions are made, karma—deserved reward or punishment—will get you in the end.

Job's belief in karma is raised only implicitly by the narrator in the first few verses, but it becomes forthright and explicit once the Accuser arrives on the scene. (As his name suggests, making accusations is precisely his role within the heavenly council.) The heavenly council gathers and a conversation ensues between Yahweh and the Accuser:

> Yahweh asked the Accuser, 'Where have you been?' And the Accuser answered Yahweh, saying, 'I've been scouring the earth as I travel around in it.'
> Yahweh asked the Accuser, 'Have you investigated my servant Job? For there is none on earth like him; he is truly a man of integrity, one who fears God and turns away from anything bad.'
> The Accuser answered Yahweh, saying, 'Does Job fear God for nothing? Have you not hedged him in on all sides, together with his house and all that he owns? You bless every work of his hands, and his cattle inundate the land! But now, stretch out your hand and strike all that belongs to him, and see if he doesn't curse you to your face!' (Job 1.7–11).

Job's righteousness is never brought into question by the Accuser. Both the narrator and God affirm Job to be a man of integrity and the Accuser says nothing to the contrary. Rather, the Accuser's charge goes deeper, insinuating that Job's behaviour, righteous though it may be, is predictable because it rests on a crude transaction with God: wealth in exchange for worship. Job's *motives* are the thing in question.

On the surface, the Accuser's accusation is directed at Job— namely, that he fears God only for his own selfish gain—but in an underhanded way the Accuser's charge is also against God for treating Job according to the principle of karma: 'Have you not hedged him in, together with his house and all that he owns—on all sides? You bless every work of his hands', and so on. The mechanistic character of Job's prayers and sacrifices is God's fault, too, because God so consistently rewards him for his supposed integrity. And isn't the Accuser right, to some degree? In fact, isn't Job's routine consistent with a biblical principle, set out quite clearly in Deuteronomy, where blessings or curses are promised as the consequences of obedience or disobedience?

In Deuteronomy, as the Israelites prepare to enter the promised land, Moses spends an entire day instructing them about how they must behave in order to establish God's kingdom in that land. As well as reminding Israel of their special role in God's purposes and underlining the importance of their laws, Moses recites to them a long list of blessings and curses, positive and negative consequences that will correspond to their behaviour in the land of Canaan. In essence, Deuteronomy is a forward-looking book that stresses the importance of Israel's choices. Consider these words of Moses:

> See, I am setting before you today a blessing and a curse: the blessing, if you obey the commandments of the Lord your God that I am commanding you today; and the curse, if you do not obey the commandments of the Lord your God, but turn from the way that I am commanding you today . . . (Deut 11.26–28 nrsv)

In Deuteronomy 28, Moses sets out the specific rewards and punishments for Israel's obedience or disobedience. And although Job himself is not an Israelite, the introduction of his character alludes to the blessings in Deuteronomy 28 in such a way that readers may understand Job's prosperity in light of those promises.[7] The following table shows how Job 1.1–3 draws on various blessings listed in Deuteronomy 28.1–14 to make the point that Job deserved his wealth; it was his rightful reward.

	Job 1.1–3	Deut. 28.1–14 (NRSV)
BLESSINGS	Once there was a man in the land of Uz, and his name was Job. This was a true man of integrity; he feared God and turned away from badness (v. 1).	If you will only obey the LORD your God, by diligently observing all his commandments (v. 1) . . . and if you do not turn aside from any of the words that I am commanding you today, either to the right or to the left . . . (v. 14a).
	And he brought into the world seven sons and three daughters (v. 2).	Blessed shall be the fruit of your womb . . . (v. 4a).
	He owned 7,000 sheep, 3,000 camels, 500 pairs of oxen, 500 donkeys, and also a huge number of servants. In fact, he was the most renowned person in the East (v. 3).	The LORD will make you abound in prosperity . . . in the fruit of your livestock (v. 11a) . . . The LORD will make you the head, and not the tail; you shall be only at the top, and not at the bottom . . . (v. 13a).

As one who fears God, Job is the father of many children and the owner of numerous flocks and herds, not to mention his status in the East where he resides happily 'at the top' (Deut. 28.13). But these positive allusions to Deuteronomy merely set the scene. For although Job continues to behave in ways that ought to secure blessings for him, he suddenly becomes the recipient of the curses of Deuteronomy 28 because of the Accuser's challenge:

	Job 1.1–3	Deut. 28.15– (NRSV)
CURSES	The oxen were ploughing and the donkeys were grazing nearby, when the Sabeans attacked them and took them (vv. 14–15).	Your ox shall be butchered before your eyes, but you shall not eat of it. Your donkey shall be stolen in front of you, and shall not be restored to you. Your sheep shall be given to your enemies, without anyone to help you (v. 31).
	The Chaldeans formed three companies and raided the camels and took them. The servants were all killed with the sword … (v. 17).	The LORD will bring a nation from far away, from the end of the earth, to swoop down on you like an eagle, a nation whose language you do not understand, a grim-faced nation showing no respect to the old or favour to the young (vv. 49–50).
	Your sons and daughters were eating and drinking wine in the house of their eldest brother, and suddenly a mighty wind came out of the desert and afflicted the four corners of the house … (vv. 18–19).	Your sons and daughters shall be given to another people, while you look on; you will strain your eyes looking for them all day but be powerless to do anything (v. 32).

In scene one, Job is described in the language of blessing; in scene three he is accursed. All of these references prepare the reader to take note of the final curse upon Job—the punchline, if you like—where the author puts subtlety aside and quotes directly from Deuteronomy 28.35:

Job 2.7	Deut. 28.35 (NRSV)
So the Accuser departed from Yahweh's presence. And he inlicted [*nakah*] Job with terrible ulcers [*shechîn ra'*] from the soles of his feet to the crown of his head.	The Lord will strike [*nakah*] you on the knees and on the legs with grievous boils [*shechîn ra'*] of which you cannot be healed, from the sole of your foot to the crown of your head.

Given the shared context of blessings and curses, the 'infliction' of 'grievous boils . . . from the sole of the foot to the crown of the head' in both Deut 28.35 and Job 2.7 hardly seems coincidental. (These are the only two occurrences of the term 'grievous boils' [NRSV] in the entire Old Testament.) But what is gained by reading Job's opening chapters with Deuteronomy 28 in mind?

These allusions to Deuteronomy's blessings and curses make it clear that Job, a paragon of righteousness, has had his lot thrown in with the wicked. The theological crux of Deuteronomy—unavoidable blessings for obedience and curses for rebellion (for which I have adopted the term 'karma' as shorthand)—is being quite deliberately turned on its head. Job has been cursed, and he is the last man on earth who deserves it. Readers, who are privy to the heavenly scenes as well as the earthly ones, know that the karmic cycle has been disrupted in order to determine whether Job serves God for God's sake or for his own selfish gain. In other words, readers have an *outside* perspective on Job's plight. But from Job's *inside* perspective, these opening chapters reflect the same frightening reality as that expressed in the first sentence of Franz Kafka's novel *The Trial*:

> FEAR OF GOD
>
> The first verse of the book of Job describes the main character with two key phrases: Job fears God and turns away from evil. It is easy enough to understand what 'turning away from evil' indicates, but what is meant by the Hebrew idiom 'to fear God'?
>
> Although the expression contains the word 'fear', fearing God is not about one's emotional state before God, but rather about making a response to God that recognizes his lordship. Walter Moberly states that '"fear of God" is the primary term within the Old Testament for depicting a true and appropriate human response to God (a Hebrew equivalent to "faith" in Christian parlance).'⁸ In the wisdom literature of the Old Testament, fearing God is closely connected with living wisely (see Job 28.28).

> Someone must have slandered Josef K., for one morning, without having done anything wrong, he was arrested.⁹

Within the world of the narrative, Job has no idea what is happening. Karma has come undone and his life has been devastated. No reason is apparent. But through the telling of a story within which a good man gets what he does not deserve, readers are invited, together with Job (and Josef K., for that matter), to search for answers in a world that has ceased to play by the rules. Who's in charge here? Why the injustice? The point of Job's story is not to suggest that God toys with his creatures. That kind of reading misses the point. Rather, the opening chapters establish Job as 'a true man of integrity' (1.1) so that we may observe how such a person will respond, especially in his God-talk, to the karmic cycle being broken.

Covered in Badness

Many readers are quite startled when they reach chapter 3 of the book of Job, almost as if they discover that they are reading a biblical version of Dr Jekyll and Mr Hyde.[10] But while it does appear that the patient and steadfast Job of chapters 1–2 suddenly morphs into a volatile, angry man who spits all his words out in a rage, we needn't draw the conclusion that these are two irreconcilable personalities. As the references to Deuteronomy 28 show, this righteous man who has habitually turned away from badness and who deserves only the richest of blessings is suddenly up to his neck in the vilest of curses! How does anyone come to terms with the sudden presence of so much evil? Job's angry outburst in chapter 3 is his gut-response to the fact that he has little control—or *no* control—over the presence of bad things in his life.

But even before we get to chapter 3, the opening chapters have a clever way of depicting how Job's relationship to 'badness' gets completely reversed. By tracing the use of the keyword *ra'* ('evil' or 'badness') in the prologue, the following development comes to light:

> Job is fundamentally opposed to *ra'* (1.1,8; 2.3).
> Job is literally covered in *ra'* (2.7).
> Job asks whether *ra'* might even come from God (2.10).
> Job earns a reputation for the *ra'* that has overcome him (2.11).

To begin with, Job is fundamentally opposed to anything and everything 'bad' (Job 1.1,8; 2.3). He turns away from it at every opportunity, not allowing its ill effects to come near him. But the boils that are inflicted upon Job as a consequence of the Accuser's wager with God are described using the same word, *ra'* (translated as 'loathsome' in the NRSV, and 'painful' in the NIV). Suddenly, through no fault of his own, Job finds himself quite literally covered 'from the sole of his foot to the crown of his head' (2.7) with the very 'badness' he has earned a reputation for avoiding. No longer can he hold the view that turning away from evil will guarantee his security, for Job's life has been overrun by numerous atrocities in a way that dramatically raises the question of God and evil. Actually, the next time the word *ra'* appears is when Job voices that very question: 'If we accept good things from the hand of God, should we not also accept bad things [*ra'*]?' (2.10). This is very different from Job's initial response: 'I left my mother's womb naked, and I will die naked. Yahweh gives and Yahweh takes away. Blessed be the name of Yahweh!' (1.21). Job has dared to ask whether God might even be the source of *ra'*. The last time *ra'* appears is in verse 11, when Job's friends arrive to comfort him for all the badness that has overcome him. Job's unexpected afflictions have turned his reputation for greatness into a reputation for badness; a classic case of poetic *in*justice, you might say.

In light of all this, it is easier to understand Job's Jekyll-and-Hyde response at the juncture between chapters 2 and 3. Job had been living under the impression that his moral integrity, prayers and sacrifices kept him a safe distance from every kind of affliction. But when the principle of karma, which he had perceived as a security system around him and his family, failed spectacularly, Job was forced to recognize that a theology of just desserts cannot always be counted on. Justice does not always prevail, and as Job's bitter lament in chapter 3 makes clear, this is extremely unsettling. At the end of Job's lengthy death-wish, he concludes:

> For the very thing I dread has happened to me;
> My worst fear has come about.
> I am not secure; I am not quiet; I am not settled;
> Disruption has come (Job 3.25–26).

What makes life so unliveable for Job after chapters 1–2 is its terrible uncertainty. How does one rest secure in such an unpredictable and unjust world? Of course, Job still believes that actions *merit* certain consequences, but justice as an ideal is very different from karma's promise that justice will always be carried out. It is Job's faith in karma—not in equity or God himself—that is unravelling.

But while Job may have lost faith in God's governance of the world, we mustn't be too quick to discard the principle of karma altogether. In one sense, karma is an appropriate way of understanding the world, provided that it is God who upholds justice and not some impersonal force. On the Bible's terms, justice is foundational to the order of God's good creation, and every creature must ultimately answer to the Creator. The Old Testament repeatedly affirms that God 'does not leave the guilty unpunished'.[11] However, that statement leaves plenty of room for God to freely determine *how* and *when* the guilty will be punished: sometimes a sinful action, e.g. an extramarital affair, has its own 'natural' consequences (Prov 6.32); sometimes a sinful action has specific consequences named by God (Gen 3.14–19); sometimes a sinful action brings about a sphere[12] of destruction upon a person's entire household (2 Sam 12.10–15); sometimes the consequences for sin are delayed because of human repentance (2 Kgs 22.19–20), and so on. Thus, Job's initial belief that people always get what they deserve in life (what I am referring to as 'karma') has some merit.

However, the link between human choices and God's response is neither as concrete nor as predictable as we would like to think, and certain forms of 'badness' force us to recognize this. Natural disasters, genetic disorders, miscarriage, cancer, and other such adversities: these hit hard upon the good as well as the bad, the innocent as well as the guilty. For whatever reasons, reality is messy,[13] and as we shall see in chapter four, this lack of orderliness in the world is a significant part of Job's gripe against God.

In his new and painful context, in which Job has been covered in badness for no apparent reason, he has begun to ask questions, and many more will follow as karma proves itself a difficult notion from which to become disentangled. But the second stage in his journey will take its cues from his so-called friends, who have much to say about why Job is suffering. In the next chapter, we turn our attention to their many words.

Dig Deeper

- Do you believe that God enforces karma (i.e. that he makes sure everyone gets what they deserve)? Explain your thoughts.

- How do you reconcile your belief in God with the injustice in the world?

- Do you ever fear God (respond to him as Lord) in order to be blessed?

- What would it look like to fear God 'for nothing'?

- When bad things happen to good people, how does this affect your trust in God?

3

Clichés

> *God helps those who help themselves.*
> ~ ANONYMOUS (not the Bible)

Suffering, Silence, Sin

Suffering is an immensely isolating experience. Nobody truly understands your situation. How can they? Even if someone else has been through a similar ordeal, they cannot possibly know what it is like to be in your shoes—*as you*. Of course, our families and communities can bring comfort, but they also have the potential to intensify painful experiences. Think about the testimonies shared in chapter one: Jamie's maimed hand led to mockery at school and a desire to do whatever it took to belong; the loss of Roslyn's baby boy led to feelings of isolation when others failed to grasp the depth and significance of her loss, suggesting carelessly that she simply 'have another one'; Wesley feared the condemnation of his peers as an adolescent, and continues to wrestle with the loneliness associated with celibacy. Like it or not, for better or worse, friends and family (and sometimes strangers) have a considerable impact on our suffering.

Lament for a Son records Nicolas Wolterstorff's grief after his 25-year-old son died in a mountaineering accident. His short but profound book contains this advice for would-be comforters:

> Your words don't have to be wise. The heart that speaks is heard more than the words spoken . . . But please: Don't say it's really not so bad. Because it is. Death is awful, demonic. If you think your task as comforter

is to tell me that really, all things considered, it's not so bad, you do not sit with me in my grief but place yourself off in the distance away from me. Over there, you are of no help. What I need to hear from you is that you recognize how painful it is. I need to hear from you that you are with me in my desperation. To comfort me, you have to come close. Come sit beside me on my mourning bench.[1]

Job's suffering is exacerbated by his family and friends. As he sits on the ash heap, grieving for his children and scraping his wounds, his wife shows no real understanding of his grief. Her advice is that Job curse God and be done with it. 'Do you still persist in your integrity?' she asks, implying that Job should know by now that no amount of good behaviour can keep trouble away. Job chides her foolishness, and nothing more is said of their relationship. But their brief exchange is sufficient to indicate that Job's bleak experience is intensified by her words. When Job's friends are introduced a few verses later, we can only hope that they will be more empathetic than his wife:

2.11 Now, when three of Job's friends heard about all this badness that had come upon him, they came, each from his place—Eliphaz the Temanite, Bildad the Shuhite, and Zophar the Naamathite. They arranged to meet together in order to come and show their sympathy and comfort him.
2.12 But when they lifted their eyes from afar, they did not even recognize him. So they lifted their voices and wailed. Each of them tore his robe, and they threw dust in the air over their heads.
2.13 And they sat with him on the ground for seven days and seven nights. But not a word was spoken to him, for they could see that his pain was excessive.

Before they famously make matters worse by opening their mouths, Eliphaz, Bildad and Zophar deserve credit for sitting in silence with Job for seven days. *Come sit beside me on my mourning bench.* Contrary to all appearances, a lot happens when we choose to be quiet and still. In the silence, our emotions rise to the surface; emotions related to doubts, anxieties, painful memories, questions, regrets, hopes, and so on. I don't doubt that the fidgeting and restlessness we feel are physical symptoms of all the subconscious mental and emotional activity. The difficulty of being quiet and sitting still is what makes the initial response of Job's friends such a rare gift. Mentioned in just a single verse, the 'seven days and nights' where 'not a word was spoken' encompasses one of the most significant developments in the book, facilitating the transition from Job's initial, automated response—'Yahweh gives and Yahweh takes away'—to his gut-wrenching cry of distress in chapter 3: 'Why didn't I die at birth?' (3.11). In the previous chapter, we observed that the defiant, ranting Job of chapter 3 seems almost like an entirely different character from the man of few words in the opening scenes. This eruption in Job's character can only have been helped along by the opportunity to sit in mutual silence with friends. It is *on the mourning bench* that Job's emotions rise to the surface and come to expression on his lips.

Once Job breaks the silence, however, his friends don't hesitate to join in the conversation. Evidently, their theological remedies for Job's plight have become like ants in their pants and they can sit still no longer. All of a sudden Job's silent friends become very vocal friends. Worse than that, they are judgmental, know-it-all friends. And yet, Eliphaz, Bildad and Zophar begin where Job began; theirs is a worldview that holds God responsible for enforcing a kind of karmic justice system. In fact, Job himself later admits that if their roles had been reversed, he might have been a 'miserable comforter' to them, just as they are to him (16.1–4). The fundamental difference between Job and his friends is that Job is in pain and they are not. Job's circumstances have raised questions for him that they have yet to consider.

A multitude of words are exchanged between Job and his friends in chapters 4–27, and I have no intention of reproducing them all here. Instead, we will focus on the conclusion that is reached (and stated repeatedly) by Eliphaz, Bildad and Zophar. Each of them, in his own way, reduces the complexity of Job's pain and suffering to a single idea: *people suffer because they have sinned*. Not very encouraging, but there it is: karma, again. At the end of the day, Job's friends fail him as friends not because they are too direct with Job, nor because they try to explain why bad things have happened to him. Job's friends let him down because they reduce his suffering to a pithy proverb, adding to his grief the misunderstanding of a community that is quick to explain his suffering but slow to enter into it with him.

Eliphaz is the first to summarize their shared conviction:

> According to what I have seen,
> people who plough iniquity and sow trouble reap the same (Job 4.8).

Later, he becomes more blunt, armed with rhetorical questions:

> Is it because of your fear of God
> that he rebukes you and judges you?
> Is it not because of your great wickedness
> and your endless sins? (Job 22.4–5)

Bildad takes the matter further, referring insensitively to the sin of Job's children as though there were no other explanation for their demise:

> Does God pervert justice?
> Does the Almighty pervert righteousness?
> When your children sinned against him,
> he handed them over to the consequence of their sin (Job 8.3–4).

In a later conversation, Bildad generalizes about how all wicked people get what is coming to them:

> Surely the light of the wicked is snuffed out,
> and the flame of his fire does not shine.
> In his tent, light is dark,
> and his lamp is snuffed out...
> He is thrust from the light into darkness
> and banished from the world (Job 18.5–6,18).

But perhaps Zophar is the most direct:

> You say, 'My teaching is right and I am pure in your sight.'
> Ha! How I wish that God would open his lips and say something to you!
> For he would proclaim to you secrets of wisdom that are
>   doubly sound.
> Know this—God has not even held all of your sin against you!
>   (Job 11.4–6)

With friends like these, as the saying goes, who needs enemies? All three 'comforters' tell Job that he is getting what he deserves, because their wisdom traditions are clear about one thing: *people suffer because they have sinned*. According to Eliphaz, Job needs only to confess that this is true and God may yet show him mercy:

> Submit yourself to him [God] and be made whole;
> that is how good things will come to you (Job 22.21).

But just as Job could not accept his wife's suggestion to 'curse God and die' he also rejects the simplistic axiom of his friends; that his sickness and losses are the consequences of sin. It is easy to identify with Job's frustration, but it is also worth pausing to ask where the friends go wrong exactly. Like Job, they believe in a God who apportions justice as each deserves, and they are right to do so. But the friends are only half-right. Their advice for Job rests on two premises:

(1) all people have sinned (Job 15.14–16)
(2) sin has consequences (Job 18.5–21; 20.4–29)

These claims are hard to dispute in themselves, but problems arise when Job's friends take things further. First, since (1) all have sinned and (2) sin has consequences, they draw the conclusion that when people suffer, it must be because they have recently committed a sin that deserves punishment. In other words, *Job is suffering because* he *has sinned*. They make no allowances for other factors in their reasoning, such as Job's outstanding integrity (which is affirmed twice by God) or the messiness and unpredictability of life.[2] They throw a blanket over the complexity of Job's situation, wrap it all up into a bundle and slap a one-size-fits-all answer on it. Second, they offer Job their cold, hard logic without empathy or warmth. One theologian has described the counsel of the friends as 'an untraumatised wisdom, not rooted in . . . the particularity of who Job is and what he has suffered.'[3] Theirs is a wisdom that hasn't been put through the wringer, a textbook response offered by people whose skin is still intact. So we are hardly surprised when Job snaps at them in frustration, 'Your memorized clichés are proverbs of ashes!' (13.12).

One Size Fits All?

Clothes labelled 'one size fits all' are unrealistic, aren't they? I'm all for a healthy dose of optimism, but *one* size fits *all*? Not likely. The same goes for those clichés people hold up like all-encompassing banners over the complexities of life. I explained earlier that I am using the term *karma* as shorthand for the principle that one always gets what one deserves. In this chapter, I use the word *cliché* as shorthand for our tendency to reduce life's conundrums to impossibly brief solutions. Sometimes we do this with short sayings and sometimes by reducing God to a more manageable theological idea. Both are problematic.

An obvious problem with short sayings is that one cliché is always bound to contradict another because each is trying to say so much. Do too many cooks spoil the broth? Or do many hands make light work? Is it better to be safe than sorry? Or is nothing ventured, nothing gained? Do good things come in small packages? Or the bigger, the better? These examples are rather trivial, but they make the point that one-size-fits-all statements cannot cover all the bases. As one saying contradicts another, we find ourselves in need of a more sophisticated worldview.

Coming up with catchy phrases that condense complex truths into a few words is not a recent fad, though. People have been doing it for centuries. Think of the aphorisms of Confucius, the sayings of the Buddha, or the proverbs of King Solomon. Even the Bible's own wisdom tradition (especially Proverbs and Ecclesiastes) includes a string of summary statements about life's big issues. But an isolated proverb from the Bible cannot be applied to all of life's wonderful complexity, either. For example, the two instructions given in Proverbs 26.4–5 are often cited for what appear to be conflicting messages:

Do not answer fools according to their folly, or you will be a fool yourself (Prov 26.4 NRSV).	Answer fools according to their folly, or they will be wise in their own eyes (Prov 26.5 NRSV).

It may well be, however, that these two proverbs have been presented side by side to make the very point that life is a more complicated business than finding short, clever sayings to live by.[4] Similarly, the structure of the book of Job warns against reducing wisdom to any single point of view. Not only are we confronted with a range of characters wielding different opinions—God, the Accuser, Job, his wife, the friends, and the narrator—but the book of Job as a whole draws on different theologies so that the reader is forced to acknowledge the tensions and get involved in the debate. We have already seen how the opening chapters of Job pick up on the theology of just desserts from Deuteronomy 28 while at the same time highlighting its shortcomings. In these ways, Job's story refutes the adage that 'one size fits all'. Only Job's friends, who have yet to experience such a profound disjuncture in their life of faith, are satisfied with a singular theology of just desserts—and to that theology they relentlessly cling.

The antagonist in *Les Misérables*, the obsessive Inspector Javert, offers a profound illustration of the dangers of a 'one size fits all' mentality. Javert is a fierce legalist whose entire life is driven by a singular obsession with upholding the law; Victor Hugo aptly describes him as a wolf with a human face.[5] To cut a very long story short, Javert spends much of his life pursuing an ex-convict named Jean Valjean who broke the law by stealing a loaf of bread to feed his sister's children. But when an unusual turn of events during the French Revolution gives Valjean the opportunity to kill the 'wolf' who has hunted him so relentlessly, Valjean frees Javert in an inexplicable act of mercy. As Javert endeavours to come to terms with what has happened, it becomes apparent that he is more a prisoner than Valjean ever was. Because of his lifelong commitment to the black-and-white letter of the law, Javert had been convinced that an ex-convict like Valjean could never amount to anything more than a rule-breaker. But as Javert catches himself feeling 'admiration for a convict,'[6] his certitude begins to crumble. Javert even questions the final authority of the law:

> His supreme anguish was the evaporation of all certainty. He felt torn up by the roots, annihilated. The code was now a mere stub in his hand . . . A whole new world appeared to his soul: kindness accepted and returned . . . leniency . . . the possibility of a tear pearling in the

eye of the law, some indefinable sense of justice according to God's rules that was the reverse of justice according to man. He saw in the darkness the terrifying sun of an unknown morality dawning; and he was appalled and dazzled by it.[7]

The undoing of Javert's 'one size fits all' belief system inflicts a certain trauma upon him. An alternative morality dawns on his soul, presenting a world where compassion reigns alongside justice, one in which the eye of the law can even shed a tear. Most profoundly, it is a world in which God's justice runs inversely to human justice. Tragically, this collision of worlds is too much for Javert, who throws himself off a bridge into the River Seine. Javert's life has been dominated by an obsession with the law for so long that in the end he finds himself unable to accommodate grace.[8] His narrow-mindedness is his downfall and his death.

We affirmed in the previous chapter that there is something of value in the notion of karma, since the Bible does indeed affirm that each will be judged according to their actions.[9] However, this theology of deservedness stands alongside other theologies within the biblical canon. Even though Job challenges the notion of a 'one size fits all' theology by disputing the reliability of karma, it is important to remember that neither Deuteronomy nor Job have the final say. Towards the end of the book of Job, when God speaks freely for himself, we are reminded that God is always more, always other, always beyond the theological categories that we set for him.

A Web of Wisdom

Developing a worldview that enables us to deal with life's complexity is no easy feat. However, it seems to me that the Bible caters to this task in a particularly profound way—as a collection of documents written by various people with a diversity of perspectives, covering a wide range of issues over an extensive period of time. Learning to hold all of the Scriptures together in a meaningful way poses its own set of challenges, though. For instance, it can be confusing after reading about violent wars in the book of Joshua to turn to Paul's letters and see references to 'the God of peace'.[10] Similarly, it can be hard to grasp how we are to understand Old Testament laws as Christians living under the new covenant. And of course, not all questions are about the relation between Old and New Testaments. 1–2 Samuel and 1–2 Chronicles offer accounts of Israel's history that appear contradictory now and then,[11] just as the gospels also sometimes differ in their chronologies.[12] But the question we are interested in here—to stay closer to our topic—is this: how should we understand Job in relation to what other books of the Bible say about God, and God's justice in particular?

In the first instance, at the risk of stating the obvious, it is important to remember that Job is *one* book of the Christian Bible. As part of a sacred collection of texts, it must be read without forgetting the other sixty-five books, many of which also have things to say about God, suffering, justice, and so on. Job's voice is one of many and his story is part of a broader narrative, a much wider web of wisdom.

Think of it this way. Picture an enormous courtroom, bustling with hundreds of Bible characters.[13] Abraham, Moses, Ruth, Esther and Daniel are there, along with many others, including Mary, John and Paul. All of these witnesses have been summoned to give testimony concerning the character of God, and one part of the proceedings, the part we are interested in, has to do specifically with God's administration of *justice* as creation's Judge and King. The room falls silent and witnesses are called upon one by one to testify concerning the God of Israel and the church. As time passes, the majority of witnesses in the courtroom offer testimonies that corroborate God's fair and reliable governance of the world. We could refer to the witness of these figures as the Bible's *core testimony* about God.

Once this core testimony has been established, however, there is still a small group of witnesses who have yet to speak. By way of *counter-testimony*, they initiate a process of cross-examination whereby Israel's core testimony about Yahweh's justice is tested for its coherence and credibility. These secondary witnesses include the psalmists of lament,[14] the so-called 'confessions' of an unhappy prophet named Jeremiah,[15] the jaded preacher of Ecclesiastes, the appropriately titled book of Lamentations, and last—though certainly not least—Job.

When all is said and done, the core testimony of Israel and the church, which affirms God's justice, remains the dominant voice in this imagined legal context, but those witnesses whose doubts and protests form a counter-testimony cannot be overlooked. I have borrowed this courtroom metaphor from Walter Brueggemann, who uses it to frame his *Theology of the Old Testament*.[16] 'What is at issue,' he says, 'is the endlessly tricky relation between "The Great Tradition" and the "little texts."'[17] One of the great strengths of the legal metaphor is its emphasis on giving each witness, whether *great* or *little,* a proper hearing.

Any number of texts from the Pentateuch and the Prophets could be quoted as examples of Israel's core testimony. But perhaps the books of Deuteronomy–2 Kings, which tell the story of how Israel became a nation in their own land, constitute the prime example of 'The Great Tradition' in the Old Testament.[18] The history begins with Moses speaking to the people about what they must do as God's chosen people in the land of Canaan and ends with the entire nation divided, conquered and exiled from their homeland(s). The authors and editors of these eight books highlight God's justice by undergirding Israel's history with a strong moral message: *the Israelites suffered because they sinned.* Sound familiar? As you can see, the theological perspective of Deuteronomy–2 Kings has much in common with the wisdom tradition of Job's friends. In fact, we could even sum up that history by borrowing a cliché from Eliphaz: 'those who plough iniquity and sow trouble reap the same' (4.8).[19]

But the controversial 'little texts' in Scripture, those witnesses in our imagined courtroom that take Job's side, must also be considered. And for their part, they testify that what you reap may in fact have nothing to do with what you have sown. The Teacher in Ecclesiastes, for instance, laments that:

> the same fate comes to all, to the righteous and the wicked, to the good and the evil, to the clean and the unclean, to those who sacrifice and those who do not sacrifice. As are the good, so are the sinners; those who swear are like those who shun an oath. This is an evil in all that happens under the sun, that the same fate comes to everyone (Eccl 9.2–3a NRSV).[20]

Or we could cite Jeremiah, who sometimes sounds very much like Job:[21]

> You will be in the right, O LORD,
> when I lay charges against you;
> but let me put my case to you.
> Why does the way of the guilty prosper?
> Why do all who are treacherous thrive? (Jer 12.1 NRSV)

As for Job himself, there is no doubt that his testimony goes against the flow. Much of what he has to say is pretty inconsistent with the Bible's overall affirmation that God is good and fair. By Job's reckoning, God perverts justice and neglects those who pursue him most rigorously! Job goes against the grain of Israel's wisdom literature (e.g. Ps 1; Prov 10) and he unsettles the claim presented in Deuteronomy–2 Kings that God punishes and rewards even-handedly. Job may be perceived as a rebel of sorts, but his questions and protests deserve a hearing, not least because God ultimately approves of his speech.

So, in answer to our question about how to understand Job in relation to what other books of the Bible say about God's justice, it is important that we attend carefully to Job's testimony even while acknowledging that his voice is one of many. As we noted above, the book of Job does not seek to replace the dominant theological voice of 'The Great Tradition'. Rather, tensions must be sustained and conflicting voices permitted to coexist without cancelling one another out. I recently saw the film *Life of Pi*, which hit home to me on this very point. (If you plan to see the film or read the book anytime soon, you should probably skip over the next paragraph to avoid spoilers.)

After the sinking of a cargo ship, Piscine Molitor Patel, known simply as Pi, endures 227 days stranded at sea. Upon his recovery from the ordeal, he is asked to give an account of what happened. He offers two versions of the story, one of them a fantastical tale involving various animals, the other a brief statement of the bare and gruesome facts. (He is compelled to offer the second account because of the response to the first: 'Mr. Patel, we don't believe your story.'[22]) After providing the second explanation, Pi is given permission to leave, but before he does he turns a question back upon his investigators (and implicitly upon the reader): 'Which is the better story, the story with animals or the story without animals?'[23] Much of the book or film's staying power hangs on this question, though actually making a choice between the two stories misses the point. Of course, in Pi's judgement, the first version—'the story with animals'—is the better one, and it undoubtedly relates some deeper truths about Pi's experience, albeit as an imaginative interpretation of his harrowing ordeal. But for readers/viewers, the two accounts must be held in tension with one another. The first contains Pi's reflections on the significance of the events, whereas the second is a raw collection of facts and not much of a story. (On its own, it would make for a dull book or film.) When asked in an interview why he called the book *Life of Pi* rather than *The Life of Pi*, Yann Martel explained, 'I deliberately left out the definite article. That would have denoted a single life.'[24] The two stories are contradictory in one sense, but we cannot understand either one properly unless we hear them both. Not only are both versions true in different ways (one as an historical record; the other as a construal of Pi's spiritual and emotional journey), but the richness of Pi's experience cannot be fully grasped unless we listen to both 'voices'.

As we noted above, biblical witnesses offer both *core testimony* (God is fair) and *counter-testimony* (God is not fair). Two responses to this observation are equally common—and equally to be avoided. One is to jump to the conclusion that different perspectives in the Bible amount to 'contradictions', and thus to conclude that the Bible is fundamentally inconsistent and flawed. But a difference in perspective is not the same as a contradiction. (Which two people perceive any aspect of life in exactly the same way, let alone their experience of God?) Actually, it is tremendously beneficial that the Bible's witness is so broad, for what single viewpoint could possibly convey all the mystery and wonder of God's character? The challenge for faith communities lies not in avoiding apparent contradictions, but in (re)discovering the implications of *each* testimony for their unique contexts.[25] The other common response is to smooth out all dissonance in an attempt to make the Bible sound more consistent. But shoving all sixty-six books of the Bible into a convenient, one-size-fits-all theology rather than honouring its form as a complex web of wisdom is also a mistake.

Instead of dismissing the biblical witness altogether or forcing it to say one thing, it is far more instructive to ask (even if it makes us nervous) why those responsible for passing on Israel's Scriptures might have chosen to preserve such a diversity of voices and traditions. Stephen Chapman posits a helpful answer to this question:

> 'Life' emerges from the *multiplicity* of voices contained within the canon, for only in the *chorus* of these voices are we able to learn to hear a voice other than our own . . . Difference within the canon is necessary if readers are to entertain other 'possible selves.'[26]

You probably recognize truth in this statement from life experience. Spending hours in conversation with others who already share your views doesn't push you out of your comfort zone. Unless we avail ourselves of voices 'other than our own', we simply reinforce what we already believe and miss out on opportunities to grow. Chapman is exactly right; variance in testimony is not just inevitable, but also desirable.

If only Job's friends understood this!

The friends get it wrong on this very issue by holding fast to traditional wisdom without taking the time to hear Job out. They do not seem to understand that taking Job seriously does not mean they have to discard their theology of just desserts altogether. Their either/or mentality is what makes them lousy friends—and poor theologians. In their narrow-mindedness, the friends not only claim to have the answers before they've heard the questions, but they take the complexities of life and the ways of God and boil them down to basic propositions. And Job is the one who suffers the consequences. His angst and confusion are not met with listening ears and he is deprived of the opportunity to talk through the theological conundrums associated with his suffering. Sadly, Job can only thump his head against an immovable wall of clichés—and keep on asking questions . . .

Dig Deeper

- What experiences of good and bad community have you had during difficult times?

- What could Job's friends have done better?

- What's wrong with clichés?

- Does it bother you that the Bible contains different perspectives?

- What other 'voices' could you be more open to?

4

Questions

I say the gods deal very unrightly with us. For they will neither (which would be best for us all) go away and leave us to live our own short days to ourselves, nor will they show themselves openly and tell us what they would have us do . . . Why must holy places be dark places?
~ C.S. LEWIS, Till We Have Faces

Are Questions the Answer?

In 2009, the Coen Brothers released the dark comedy, *A Serious Man*, which bore numerous similarities to the book of Job. The film's main character is Larry Gopnik, a Jewish physics professor, whose life is falling apart around him. As his problems worsen, Larry seeks advice from three rabbis. The first, a man clearly too young to have any real life experience, suggests simply that Larry change his perspective. Responding to the turmoil of Larry's situation, the young rabbi retorts, 'This is life. You have to see these things as expressions of God's will. You don't have to like it, of course.' Larry, in turn, grins reluctantly and acknowledges, 'The boss isn't always right, but he's always the boss.'

Certain passages in Scripture reflect this kind of attitude; God is the boss and what the boss says is final. For instance, in the sixth-century BC when God released the Israelites from their captivity in Babylon, he did so by raising up a foreign Messiah.[1] Needless to say, this raised some Israelite eyebrows. *Our Messiah is not one of us?* Through the prophet Isaiah, therefore, God asserted his right to act outside of human expectations, based on the simple fact that he is the Potter, the Creator, the Boss:

> Woe to those who quarrel with their Maker,
>   those who are nothing but potsherds
> among the potsherds on the ground.
> Does the clay say to the potter,
>   'What are you making?' (Isa 45.9 NIV)

Israel is likened to broken pieces of pottery at their Potter's feet who dare to rebuke their Maker and question his purposes. The absurdity of the image makes Isaiah's point nicely. God responds to some of Job's protests in a similar vein:

> Does a prosecutor bring a case against God? (Job 40.2a)

> Would you even undo my decree?
> Do you condemn me in order to justify yourself? (Job 40.8)

Questions arise in Israel and Job for the same reason that they arise for many of us: because God behaves in ways we don't understand.[2] However, trying to squeeze God into boxes of our own design, labelled 'fair' and 'right', denies God his freedom and otherness. This is especially the case when we put God in the wrong to prove ourselves right (Job 40.8). It is not up to the creature to dictate how the Creator behaves. Or, as Larry Gopnik puts it to the young rabbi, God is 'always the boss' regardless of whether or not we agree with him.

This is not the whole story, though, for as we know, Job pushes past quiet resignation and demands that God answer his questions. The Coen Brothers reflect a similar dynamic in *A Serious Man*. By the time Larry Gopnik sees the second rabbi, he is insistent that God respond:

> Rabbi Nachtner: 'These questions that are bothering you, Larry, maybe they're like a toothache. You feel them for a while, then they go away.'
> Larry: 'I don't want them to just go away. I want an answer!'
> Rabbi Nachtner: 'Sure! We all want the answer. But Hashem[3] doesn't owe us the answer, Larry. Hashem doesn't owe us anything. The obligation runs the other way.'
> Larry: 'Why does he make us feel the questions if he's not going to give us any answers?'
> Rabbi Nachtner: 'He hasn't told me.'

When Job's circumstances cause him to 'feel the questions', he enquires about the relationship between God and evil: 'If we accept good things from the hand of God, should we not also accept bad things?' (2.10). Perhaps our first instinct upon hearing such a question is to determine whether the correct answer is 'yes' or 'no', but the real importance of Job's query lies not in whatever answer he (or we) would give it, but in the fact that Job dared to speak it at all. Job's fundamental posture in life has shifted from settledness and certainty to an open consideration of alternative possibilities. Throughout the numerous conversations that follow, as Job's friends try to convince him that he is suffering because of sin, questions continue to play a central role in Job's endeavour to understand where he stands before God. When he is assured by Bildad that God will not reject a person of integrity, Job asks, 'But what makes a man righteous before God?' (9.2). When Eliphaz tells him how deeply sinful he is, Job asks, 'Where then, is my hope?' (17.15). In a disagreement with Zophar about whether the wicked get their just desserts or live long, happy lives, Job raises yet another pertinent question: 'How often is the lamp of the wicked extinguished?' (21.17a). Undergirding all of these enquiries is Job's frustration with God for refusing to comply with human expectations: Job's integrity no longer seems to matter to God; the basis for his hope is gone; the wicked don't get what they deserve. Job's questions express deep agitation, but as we shall see, they may also be understood as part of the *answer* to his own predicament.

In the dialogues between Job and his friends, Job's language is raw and argumentative, but he does not rant as a new convert to atheism who wants the world to know about it. He may have doubts about God's ways and even God's goodness, but not once does Job doubt God's existence. On the contrary, Job's quarrel with God could hardly have arisen were it not for their long-standing relationship. This is crucial for a proper understanding of the book of Job. The same thing may be said of the Psalms, which functioned as a kind of hymn book for ancient Israel. The book of Psalms contains too many laments for us to think that asking questions of God has no place in the communal, spiritual life of God's people. (Out of the 150 psalms, more than a third are classified as laments.) But it is significant that lament psalms are part of Israel's *worship*. That is to say, the kind of questioning commended in these psalms (and in Job) is not aimless, angry venting, but rather an honest attempt to engage with a personal God in order to better understand what he is doing in our lives. The questions are personal and prayerful. When Job's beliefs and experiences come into conflict, he is bold enough to voice his uncertainty. Later, we will see that this kind of authenticity is pleasing to God.

Questions can lead us from stale assumptions into new territory, and while some Bible texts encourage us to trust God even when we don't understand his actions, modes of speech that press God for answers are also affirmed in the Bible. The attitudes of self-abandonment and self-assertion[4] must be held together in the context of our life with God. Although greater emphasis is given to self-assertion in the book of Job, the story surprisingly concludes with God affirming Job for speaking 'rightly' (42.7–8). We will look more closely at what this means in the next chapter; suffice it to say at this point that Job's 'bold speech of assault is in fact received at the throne not as disobedience but as a new kind of obedience.'[5] His questions, as a kind of wrestling with God, lead directly to a life-changing conversation with God in the whirlwind.

Wrestling with God: Rounds 1, 2 & 3

Jacob is a biblical character who is well known for having some success in a wrestling match with God. After being estranged from his elder brother Esau for many years (due to stealing his birthright), Jacob is finally on his way home to make amends when he is met by a mysterious figure on the banks of the Jabbok river, who wrestles with him through the night. Hours pass as they grapple and fight, each vying for the upper hand. Eventually, as the sun begins to rise and Jacob's mysterious opponent realizes that he cannot win, he strikes Jacob's hip, putting it out of joint. Even then, however, Jacob refuses to release his grip until he receives a blessing. His determination wins out and Jacob is renamed: 'You shall no longer be called Jacob, but Israel, for you have striven with God and with humans, and have prevailed' (Gen 32.28 NRSV). From the way Jacob's story is told, it is apparent that both his limp and his new identity are evidence of the same painfully transformative process.[6]

Job's struggle with God is not presented as a physical feat but as a verbal debate, where blows are struck with metaphors, ideas and words. And to be sure, Job holds no punches. He makes a number of accusations against God's character in general, as well as various allegations about how God has treated him in particular. According to Job, God does not control his anger (9.13); he mocks the despair of the innocent (9.23); he blindfolds judges to pervert justice (9.24); he deprives world leaders of the ability to reason (12.24); he destroys hope (14.19); and he charges no one with wrongdoing (24.12). One might well ask what godly qualities are left to speak of! Equally harsh are the accusations concerning God's treatment of Job himself: God has seized Job by the neck to crush him (16.12); drawn a net around him (19.6); counted him as an enemy (19.11); and alienated Job's friends from him (19.13). Evidently, 'the witness of the book of Job is that rage and even blame directed at God are valid moments in the life of faith.'[7]

It is not surprising, then, that Job's struggle with God is presented in the language of a courtroom. The words 'judgement', 'case', 'argue' and 'decide' occur regularly throughout the speeches, as well as questions like, 'What charges do you have against me?' (10.2b). In fact, given the cyclical form of the speeches and their content, it has been suggested that the book of Job presents a lawsuit drama where Job is the prosecutor, God the defendant, and Job's friends act as judges and witnesses.[8] The legal metaphor appropriately highlights the serious implications of Job's protest.

One of the most noticeable changes throughout the three cycles of speeches (or three rounds of wrestling, depending on which metaphor you prefer) is the way in which Job addresses God. In the first cycle, Job often addresses God directly, using the second-person pronoun 'you', but this decreases dramatically in the second cycle and then stops altogether in the third. It is clear even from just a quick glance at the graph opposite that Job finds it difficult to keep addressing a God who won't answer. In the next few pages, we will explore some of Job's rhetorical ploys to evoke a response from God.

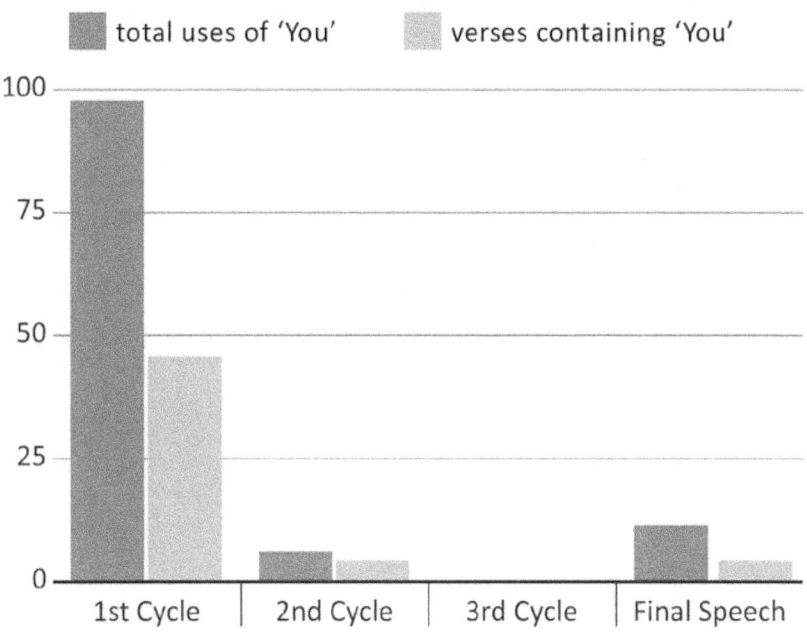

Job's words addressed to God[9]

As many of us know from watching a bit of TV drama, one sure way to win the jury over is to catch the defendant out by using their own testimony against them. That well-known scene from *A Few Good Men* (1992) comes to mind where Col. Jessup (played by Jack Nicholson), who is on trial for giving an order that resulted in the death of a marine, exposes his guilt by shouting angrily at the young defence lawyer, 'You can't handle the truth!' On more than one occasion during the first cycle of speeches (chs 4–14), Job turns Israel's testimony about God against him by alluding to the Psalms. 'Savaging the words of a traditional prayer or hymn can often be a way of expressing the painful sense that God has betrayed the relationship,'[10] writes Carol Newsom, who refers to such texts as 'anti-psalms'. In Psalm 8, for instance, God is praised for caring so deeply for mere mortals, for being 'mindful of them' (8.4 NRSV). Job turns this sentiment into a sarcastic taunt, asking why God must be so *unrelenting* in his 'mindfulness':

> What are human beings, that you make so much of them,
> that you set your mind on them,
> that you watch them every morning,
> and investigate them at every moment?
> Can't you divert your gaze from me,
> and leave me alone long enough to swallow my spittle?
> (Job 7.17–19)

Psalm 139 is another well-known psalm that praises God for carefully knitting together each and every human being in their mother's womb. Once again, Job takes this hopeful image and puts his own spin on it as God's prosecutor, saying:

> Your hands, which crafted and made me,
> also crush me.
> Please remember that you shaped me like clay!
> Will you return me to dust?
> Wasn't it you who poured me out like milk
> and curdled me like cheese?
> You put skin and flesh upon me,
> and knit me together with bones and sinews (Job 10.8–11).

After knitting me together with such care, how can you now destroy me so easily? Job's inquisition is brave, and with the world's Maker as his opponent he knows his chances of success are slim. In fact, with God as his indomitable foe *and* judge, Job fears that any response he does manage to evoke from God is not likely to be very sympathetic. He imagines that God will simply overwhelm him with a storm (9.17)—which is not a bad guess, as it turns out.[11] But even in spite of feeling that the odds are stacked against him, unlike his friends who speak *about* God with distanced objectivity, Job keeps directing his questions *to* God:

> Why have you made me your target? (7.20b)

> Tell me, on what grounds do you charge me? (10.2b)

> Why do you hide your face,
> and regard me as your enemy? (13.24)

Once we reach the second cycle of speeches (chs 15–21), however, considerably fewer of Job's words are directed to God. This reflects a dynamic many can relate to. When it feels as though God is against us or is hiding his face, it becomes increasingly difficult to break the silence. After losing his wife of just three years to cancer, C.S. Lewis speaks candidly about the challenge of addressing a God who feels absent:

> Meanwhile, where is God? ... When you are happy ... you will be — or so it feels — welcomed with open arms. But go to him when your need is desperate, when all other help is vain, and what do you find? A door slammed in your face, and a sound of bolting and double bolting in the inside. After that, silence. You may as well turn away. The longer you wait, the more emphatic the silence will become.[12]

As prayer becomes increasingly difficult for Job in the second and third cycles of speeches, he adopts an alternative form of rhetoric for engaging with God. Direct, personal prayer is replaced by Job's desperate plea for an advocate to speak on his behalf. As his friends repeatedly feed him the same cliché—*you are suffering because of your sin*—Job calls for a 'witness' and 'advocate' (16.19), a 'redeemer' (19.25) and an 'honest person' (23.7) to reason with God on his behalf. (Not until the end of his final speech does Job demand a response from the Judge himself; see 31.35). In spite of how difficult it is to contend with a God who seems to disappear when things get tough, Job is to be commended—and in the end *will* be commended—for persisting in his attempts to communicate with God. Even when he struggles to articulate his questions to God directly, Job continues to wrestle with the issue of justice, asking why the principle of karma is not applied to the wicked:

> Why do the wicked go on living,
>   growing old and staying strong?
> Their descendants are established in their presence,
>   their offspring before their eyes.
> Their homes are at peace and without fear;
>   the rod of God's discipline is not upon them.
> Their bulls breed without fail,
>   their cows give birth without miscarrying.

> They release their children like a flock;
>> and their offspring dance about.
> They sing to the tambourine and harp,
>> and rejoice to the music of the flute.
> They spend their years in prosperity
>> and descend peacefully to Sheol [the world of the dead].
> But to God they say, 'Let us be!
>> We take no pleasure in knowing your ways.
> Who is the Almighty, that we should serve him?
>> And what do we gain from praying to him?'
> But their prosperity is not even their own doing!
>> (The way of the wicked is far removed from me.)
> How often is the lamp of the wicked extinguished?
> How often does calamity come upon them?
> How often does he, in his anger, give them their share of sorrow? (Job 21.7–17)

Like his three friends, Job believes that the righteous ought to prosper and the wicked ought to suffer. And now that this 'rule' has been broken in his own life, Job is beginning to see it all around him. Moreover, if Job is right and God does indeed treat the wicked and the righteous in the same way,[13] then he is justified in asking what the wicked stand to gain by praying (21.15). Since the wicked already have everything they could possibly want, why bring God into the equation? The same could be said for the righteous; if God treats everyone alike, why pray? The irony, however, is that whatever doubts Job may have about prayer, he himself does not stop praying. Even as he addresses God less in the second cycle of speeches (chs 15–21) and not at all in the third (chs 22–27), he continues to trust against all the evidence that God is present in the midst of his pain. God may not be present in a way that offers Job much comfort, but Job would sooner believe that God is capricious than cease believing in him altogether. After all three speech cycles, Job turns his face toward heaven one last time, just long enough to shout out to God in despair:

> I cry out for your attention, but you do not answer me!
> I have taken a stand, but you just look at me!
> You have turned on me cruelly;

with the force of your hand you persecute me!
You lift me up and throw me to the wind,
You toss me about in the storm.
And I know that you are bringing about my death,
to that house appointed for all the living (Job 30.20–23).

In Job's mind, God is no longer merely ignoring him. God has become his Enemy. 'You have turned on me cruelly . . . you persecute me!' Such harsh accusations combined with an insistence on speaking directly to God seem almost incompatible, but this tension is 'intended not just to modify our view of a certain righteous man but to redefine the concept of righteousness itself.'[14] As he faces up to God in protest, Job's integrity, already recognized in the opening verse of the book, takes on new depths. Like Jacob, Job has wrestled with God and prevailed. But before we see how God blesses *this* stubborn opponent, we must first hear Job's final speech, the rhetorical peak of his struggle against God.

Dust and Ashes

What is Job's fundamental gripe against his Maker? Is there one main question that drives his lawsuit against God? A brief look at Job's final speech in chapters 29–31 reveals that the crux of the matter remains unchanged. Job's biggest question is still the karma question: *How can this be happening to me when I have done nothing to deserve it?* The speech divides into three parts (one for each chapter) which coordinate to express Job's most daring accusation against God yet.

First, in chapter 29, Job offers a portrait of himself in his heyday, when all was well between him and the world:

If only I could return to months gone by:
    to days of divine providence,
    when his lamp shone over my head
    and by his light I would walk in darkness;
    as I was at my peak,
    when the protection of God was over my tent;
    when the Almighty was still with me,
    and my children were all around me (Job 29.2–5).

And so he continues, revelling in pleasant memories from days gone by. This reminiscence of the past is then set in contrast with chapter 30, where Job describes how badly he is treated in the present, now that God has abandoned him:

> But now I am the subject of their scornful song;
> I am a word of warning to them.
> They are disgusted by me, they stay away from me;
> they do not hold back from spitting in my presence[15] (Job 30.9–10).

The contrast between the well-respected Job of chapter 29 and the disrespected Job of chapter 30 lays the groundwork for Job's main point in chapter 31, which begins with a clear statement of what he expects from God:

> And what allotment from God above?
> What inheritance from the Almighty on high?
> Isn't ruin for the unrighteous?
> And tragedy for troublemakers? (Job 31.2–3)

The words 'allotment' and 'inheritance' indicate that Job's primary concern is with entitlement; Job wants what he deserves from God. And given his convictions (stated in verse 3), Job is at a loss to understand the tragic reality of his situation. Job the righteous peacemaker has been inflicted with the ruin that belongs to unrighteous troublemakers; again, we are reminded of how the blesses and curses of Deuteronomy 28 have been reversed. For the rest of the chapter, Job makes the point that nothing is as it should be. He sets out a long list of hypothetical reasons why God might have been justified for humiliating him in this way—the point being that he has done none of the things in the list:

> If I proceeded with falsehood . . . (31.5)
> If my step strayed from the path . . . (31.7)
> If my heart was seduced by a woman . . . (31.9)
> If I rejected the cause of my male or female slaves . . . (31.13)
> If I denied the desires of the poor . . . (31.16)
> If I saw anyone perish for lack of clothing . . . (31.19)
> If I raised my hand against the orphan . . . (31.21)

> If I put my confidence in gold . . . (31.24)
> If I rejoiced because my wealth was great . . . (31.25)
> If I rejoiced at the ruin of those who hated me . . . (31.29)
> If I covered up my sins, as other people do . . . (31.33)

By the end of chapter 31, Job's point has been made with resounding clarity: as a reward for his complete devotion to God, Job has inherited complete devastation! It is clear that Job has lost faith in God's implementation of justice, but what does he hope will come of this final, desperate plea? What does he actually want?

Job's complaints have often been understood as though he were asking God for a reasoned response to the problem of human suffering, but there is something deeper and more personal at stake here. Job used to be respected, but now he is mocked and assaulted; he used to be sought out for his wisdom, but now he is called a fool; he used to confront injustice to save the innocent, but now his own cries for help are ignored. Does he want an explanation for all this? Surely he has had enough of explanations at this point! No, Job has been utterly humiliated and this is his last-ditch effort to salvage some dignity. Job wants vindication because his entire community has drawn the wrong conclusions from his suffering. Having witnessed all the tragedy in his life, they have read between the lines according to the law of karma[16] and turned their backs on a man they once held in high regard. In their eyes, Job now walks among them as a 'word of warning' (30.9). Once again, we see how painful circumstances can be exacerbated by those around us. And to add insult to injury, one of the most painfully ironic things about all this is that Job used to be the very one who spoke up for those in need of an advocate:

> Didn't I weep for those whose day was hard?
> Didn't my soul grieve for those in need?
> But when I hoped for something good, evil came;
> and when I waited for light, darkness came (Job 30.25–26).

Now that Job is suffering, no one will give him a hearing. He has lost his voice and become invisible to his community, and he simply cannot understand why God has permitted his life to fall from the heights of chapter 29 to the depths of chapter 30. In fact,

Job holds God responsible for more than just neglect. At the heart of his speech, Job describes various youths in his community who mock and push him around, taking advantage of his weakness (30.12–15). But as his rhetoric reaches its crescendo, his complaint takes an unexpected turn, for it is not the youths who grab Job by the neck and throw him to the ground, but God! God is identified as the leader of these bullies who taunt Job in his weakness:

> With great power, he disguises himself in my clothing;
> he grabs me by the neck of my tunic.[17]
> He has hurled me into the clay,
> and I have become like dust and ashes (Job 30.18–19).

Job's oppression at the hands of irreverent youths throughout chapter 30 is finally expressed as persecution at the hands of God, who approaches Job disguised in familiar garments (presumably to gain his trust), but then grabs Job by the neck and scatters him to the wind 'like dust and ashes.' This imagery of a bully was also used of God earlier:

> I was at peace, and he destroyed me;
> he grabbed me by the neck and pummelled me.
> He made me stand as his target (Job 16.12).

While this is not the first time Job has used violent turns of phrase, on this occasion Job's harsh descriptions of mistreatment are combined with references to creation in order to make the point that his life is being

---

DUST AND ASHES

The phrase 'dust and ashes' appears only three times in the OT, twice in the book of Job (30.19; 42.6) and once in Genesis 18. In all three contexts, human beings address God on the subject of justice. In Genesis 18, Abraham boldly expresses his concern about the righteous and the wicked being treated alike, and some of his words could just as easily have come from Job's mouth: 'Far be it from you to do such a thing, to slay the righteous with the wicked, so that the righteous fare as the wicked! Far be that from you! Shall not the Judge of all the earth do what is just?' (Gen 18.25 NRSV; see Job 9.22). In spite of his boldness, however, Abraham recognizes the implausibility of his situation; a mere mortal—'I who am but dust and ashes' (18.27 NRSV)—standing face to face with his Creator and daring to offer counsel about how creation might be justly governed. The parallels between Abraham and Job reinforce the meaning of the phrase 'dust and ashes' as an acknowledgement of human frailty, even insignificance, before God.

undone by his Creator. In an earlier lament that we compared with Psalm 139,[18] Job mentioned clay, from which human beings are formed, and dust, to which we all return:

> Your hands, which crafted and made me,
> also crush me.
> Please remember that you shaped me like clay!
> Will you return me to dust? (Job 10.8–9)

Similarly, here at the high point of his case against God, Job speaks of being *unmade* at the hands of his Maker. Job's imaginative turns of phrase teeter on the edge of blasphemy, revealing that he feels utterly betrayed by a God he has been led to trust. For Job to say, 'I have become like dust and ashes' is to mourn the loss of his dignity as a person made in God's image. It is a powerful way of lamenting the undeserved reversal of his fortunes, the utter injustice of his plight, and his humiliation upon the ash heap amidst a community that once respected and loved him. God, the cosmic bully, has grabbed Job by the collar and thrown him back into the mud from which he was formed. His entire existence has been capsized by God's inexplicable grudge against him.

These three chapters (29–31) offer a clear presentation of Job's case: *God does not govern the world in such a way that human behaviour is fairly met with reward or punishment, and Job's unmaking is a direct consequence of this.* In Job's mind, creation is badly designed at best, completely broken at worst. Needless to say, the Creator is accountable for this state of affairs and Job thinks it is high time he said something about it:

> Who will give me a hearing?
> Look, here is my signature . . . Let the Almighty answer me!
> (Job 31.35a)

Dig Deeper

- If you could ask God any question and get an immediate response, what would you ask?

- How do you respond when God does not act in accordance with your expectations?

- What is significant about the fact that a third of the Psalms are laments?

- Have you ever felt angry with God? How do you express that anger?

- What can we learn from Job's way of engaging with God?

5

Conversation

> *The most important thing in communication is hearing what isn't said.*
> ~ PETER DRUCKER

Goats and Asses

In the last verse of Job 31, the narrator informs readers that Job's words have come to an end; the prosecution needs a rest! The first verse of Job 32 announces that Job's friends have had enough, too. 'So these three men stopped responding to Job, because he was righteous in his own eyes' (32.1). At this impasse a new character named Elihu interjects angrily. After waxing eloquent for some time about his grandiose intentions to correct the error of Job's ways, Elihu goes on to say . . . well, nothing new really. One almost gets the sense that his primary contribution is to provide some comic relief, an intermission, before Yahweh's incoming storm. Elihu's speech ends with a nice bit of irony, too. Just as he reaches his rhetorical peak with a definitive statement that human beings cannot encounter God Almighty (37.23), he is interrupted by none other than God Almighty! And while the narrator makes it clear that God has shown up to answer Job, God's opening words surely ring in Elihu's ears as well:

> Who is this, casting a shadow over wisdom with ignorant speech?
> Now make yourself ready!
> I will question you, and you will answer me! (38.2–3)

Will God finally tell Job about his wager with the Accuser? Will he give a (theo)logical response to the problem of human pain? Will he state that Job does, in fact, deserve everything that has befallen him? As you probably know, God says none of these things. After more than thirty chapters of words, words, words, each of them laid down like bricks in an attempt to build up walls that constrain and define God, the Creator appears in a storm to devastate the parameters established for him by his creatures. Job's insistent questioning has finally found an audience with God, but now he must brace himself for the encounter.

One doesn't need a degree in pastoral care to see that Yahweh's response lacks sensitivity. In fact, it even seems that God is *trying* to disorient Job—not in a cruel attempt to diminish his worth, but in order that God may reorient him to his actual place in the grand scheme of things.[1] Maybe this is why God speaks from a whirlwind; an unpredictable force of nature is the perfect complement to God's flurry of hard-hitting questions: Who is this . . . ? (38.2) Where were you . . . ? (38.4) Who measured the earth? (38.5) Who restrained the sea? (38.8) Have you commanded the sunrise? (38.12), and so on. It may seem odd to refer to chapters 38–41 as God's *answer*, given the extent to which his speech is driven by questions (no less than seventy of them in the NIV!). But the investigative pattern of God's response underlines an important part of its message: human beings answer to God, not vice versa. God is the Centre, not Job.

Even so, why all this talk of weather conditions and wild animals? Hasn't God been listening to Job's cries of distress? Is he choosing to ignore Job's concerns altogether? Or is something else going on here? Throughout the cycles of speeches, Job has railed against God for failing to maintain order and for permitting a righteous man to suffer. God's answer may strike us as confusing and disappointing at first, but if we listen carefully, it is precisely these issues of *order* and *entitlement* that God proceeds to address.

First, God boasts about the grandeur of the cosmos (38.1–38). Oceans, clouds, thunder and rain, boundaries for the mighty seas, the perfect balance of light and dark, starry constellations—all of it awaits God's command. This dramatic portrait of the world is thrust upon Job to assert that God is quite capable of managing the universe. His power is limitless and he certainly doesn't need Job's 'ignorant speech' (38.2) to keep things in order. God then zooms in on the peculiar characteristics of various creatures as evidence: the lion, the raven, the mountain goat, the deer, the wild ass . . . to name but a few. The mention of so many animals seems a little haphazard, but God's point is that much of creation—like its Creator—is untamed and untameable.[2] Again, Job's notions of orderliness do not apply.

'Do you know when mountain goats give birth?' asks Yahweh (39.1). Since mountain goats live far from towns and cities and exist largely outside of people's purview, it is unlikely that Job knows anything at all about their breeding or birthing habits. And of course, that is exactly the point. These goats deliver their young without the knowledge (or assistance) of humans, and they do so successfully. God alone knows their seasons and watches over their welfare. And they are not the only undomesticated animals that thrive apart from human principles of order:

> Who set the wild ass free?
> Who loosened the bonds of the swift ass,
> to which I have given the desert as a home,
> the salt flats as her dwelling place?
> She mocks the chaos of the city;
> she does not heed the shouts of a driver.
> She explores the mountains as her pasture,
> seeking anything green (Job 39.5–8).

Cities are the pride of human beings in their need for systems and structure, but the wild ass mocks the chaos of city life. No sounds of oppression ('the shouts of a driver') will ever tyrannize this animal because she is not subject to humanity's ordering of the world. Like the mountain goat, the wild ass is free because God has made it so. The same can also be said for wild oxen (39.9–12), ostriches (39.13–18), horses (39.19–25) and birds of prey (39.26–30). These verses present a kind of *National Geographic* picture gallery of what it looks like to be free from the transactions of human society. God's intention is hardly that people ought to behave more like these animals. Rather, the message conveyed is that God's wise ordering of creation will never be fully evident to humanity.

Job, like many of us, would prefer it if God managed the world in ways that were more predictable. If it were up to Job, he would take certain aspects of God's good character, such as the allocation of justice according to people's just desserts (i.e. karma), and make them into hard-and-fast rules; the wicked would *always* suffer and the righteous would *always* prosper. A more transactional ordering of creation like that would make things so much more manageable—and more *controllable*. But it would also turn God into a puppet. Such a God would no longer be free and could no longer be called a Person. In response to Job, then, God describes various wild animals that thrive within God's design, even though—perhaps even *because*—they cannot be tamed to conform to human expectations. God knows what he is doing, even if the wisdom of his ways is not always perceptible to us.

Similarly, Job's final speech (ch's 29–31) is built on the assumption that God ought to dish out reward and punishment in accordance with deeds (see pp. 57–61). But what if *deservedness* is not the bottom line for God? What if God is content 'to bring rain upon a land where no one lives, on an uninhabited desert' (38.26)? What if God is like a landowner who doesn't feel obligated to pay the workers in his vineyard according to their notions of justice, their standards of who deserves more or less pay? What if, to those who worked longer and on that basis assumed that they were entitled to more pay, God simply replied:

> 'Take what belongs to you and go; I choose to give to this last the same as I give to you. Am I not allowed to do what I choose with what belongs to me? Or are you envious because I am generous?' So the last will be first, and the first will be last (Matt 20.14–16 NRSV).

The last will be first and the first will be last? What kind of God treats people like this? Clearly, one who refuses to conform to human conventions and expectations. In a podcast I was listening to recently, I was struck by this description of God's unfamiliar ways:

> In the upside-down kingdom of God,
>   weakness is strength,
>   humility is authority,
>   giving is receiving,
>   peacemaking is heroism,
>   sacrifice is love,
>   and forgiveness is success.[3]

This is a God who cannot be tamed to inhabit an anthropocentric (human-centred) universe. Rather, he is a God who inhabits his own Theocentric (God-centred) space, a God whose ways are beyond our ways, a God who gives and blesses 'for nothing'. If God's whirlwind response makes one thing clear, it is that *he blesses freely and abundantly, but not according to any human system that would mechanize his grace*. Job has been confronted with a disturbing reality: a world in which God exercises his freedom in ways that make little sense to humanity. How does one respond to such a revelation?

A Change of Mind

We are finally in a position to consider the impact of Yahweh's overwhelming response. Job responds twice to God, once in the middle of God's speech and then again at its conclusion. Although both responses are brief, they are critical for our understanding of the book as a whole. On the first occasion, Job acknowledges how very small he is in the grand scheme of things. God's barrage of questions and cosmological boast seem to have put Job in his place:

> 40.3 And Job answered Yahweh, saying,
> 40.4 'Look, I am so small! What can I say to you?
>   I put my hand over my mouth.
> 40.5 I spoke once, but I'm not going to respond
>   —even twice, but I won't do it again.

At that point, however, God had not finished speaking and Job's feeble apology was quashed. God still had much to say about the Behemoth (ch. 40) and the Leviathan (ch. 41), two untameable creatures of which God seems especially proud. Only after God has spoken at length about these fearless and powerful beasts does Job get the opportunity to speak up again:

> 42.1 And Job answered Yahweh, saying:
> 42.2 'I know that you can do all things,
>   and that none of your purposes can be frustrated.
> 42.3 "Who is this, obscuring wisdom through a lack of knowledge?"
>   [see 38.2]

> It was me who spoke—but without understanding—
> of things that are beyond me, which I do not know about.
> 42.4 "Now listen, and I will speak;
> I will question you, and you will answer me!" [see 38.3]
> 42.5 As a report to the ear, I had heard of you,
> but now my eye sees you.
> 42.6 Therefore I reject,
> and change my mind about, "dust and ashes."' [see 30.19]

Job begins by acknowledging the limitless power and inexorable purposes of God (42.2). For better or worse, God can do what God wants. Then, couched between two quotations[4] from Yahweh's barrage of questions, Job admits that he has ventured further than his understanding should have permitted (42.3–4). But the real substance of Job's response is in Job 42.5–6. In these two verses, Job discloses the tremendous impact that God's self-revelation has had upon him. It is important to notice also that verses 5–6 are joined by the word 'therefore'. As my grandfather used to tell me, 'Paul, when you're reading the Bible and you see the word "therefore", you need to ask what it is *there for*.' In this case, Job's change of mind in verse 6 rests squarely on whatever he 'sees' in verse 5. But let's slow down and give these verses the close attention they deserve:

> 42.5 As a report to the ear, I had heard of you,
> but now my eye sees you.
> 42.6 Therefore I reject,
> and change my mind about, 'dust and ashes.' [see 30.19]

What exactly is Job referring to in verse 5? Our best clue is that he makes a comparison between two perceptions of God: *what he had heard from others in the past and what he sees for himself in the present.* By comparing Job's past and present, perhaps we can grasp more precisely what has happened to him.

From the prologue and Job's own words, we know that in the past Job perceived himself to be the deserving centre. God had always been a very important part of his world, but a *part* of *Job's* world, nonetheless. Job's prayers and sacrifices had been met with security and prosperity, and he had happily feared God from that privileged position.

Then came that moment when *life as you know it ends*.

The deaths of all his children, the desolation of his entire estate, the loss of physical wellbeing, the antagonism of his wife and friends, the judgmental sneers of his community and the disruption of Job's identity[5]—all of this dislodged Job from his settled existence at the centre and cast him to the fringes. This is not to say that Job had previously been oblivious to suffering altogether. Sure, he had reached down from his favourable position to help those in his community who needed it. In fact, he had done so regularly. But he had never been in their shoes. He had never seen the world from *that* place—until now. But once Job's deep, personal anguish makes it possible for him to view life from another angle altogether, God's unsettling response then reinforces what Job's painful circumstances have already begun to teach him: that Job is not the deserving centre. In response to Job's complaint about his inverted inheritance (31.2–4), God speaks through a(nother) whirlwind to give Job the closest thing to an answer that he is going to get: a vision of God as the True Centre.

This, I believe, is what Job testifies to seeing in 42.5. God has made himself known as the One from whom all else takes its bearings, and Job's perspective has been altered dramatically. As Job himself puts it, 'Look, I am so small!' (40.4). Job's epiphany strikes me as being somewhat comparable to the Copernican Revolution. The discovery of Nicolas Copernicus (1473–1543) displaced, or quite literally de-centred, the very world we live in when he determined that the planets do not rotate around the earth as had previously been assumed, but around the sun. Needless to say, his discovery had enormous implications both for science and religion.[6]

Job's case against God had rested on the assumption that Job's notions of happiness, justice and entitlement were the gravitational core around which everything else revolved. That was what led him, at the peak of his argument, to identify God as a bully (30.18–21). But a conclusion like that is only inevitable when we expect a loving and powerful God to behave according to *our* ideals. God is perceived as a generous Santa Claus when we get what we want, and as a bully when we suffer. Job makes this very transition between chapter 1, where his prayers and sacrifices are rewarded, and chapter 30, where he accuses God of throwing him to the ground. In reality, though, God is neither Santa in the sky nor the world's biggest bully. He is only perceived as such because of Job's (and our) problematic vantage point. In response to Job's complaint, therefore, God affirms a simple but radical truth: God, and not humanity, is the Centre. As offensive as these words will always sound to human ears, *the world does not revolve around us.* That is why God's excursion to the zoo in chapters 38–41 catches us off-guard. I like the way Jon Levenson, professor of Jewish studies at Harvard, sums up God's scathing response from the whirlwind:

> The brunt of that harangue is that creation is a wondrous and mysterious place that baffles human assumptions and expectations because it is not anthropocentric but theocentric. Humanity must learn to adjust to a world not designed for their benefit and to cease making claims (even *just* claims) upon its incomprehensible designer and master.[7]

Rather than answering Job within his limited framework, God liberates him by expanding his field of vision. Thus, as Job declares in 42.5, it is only *now*, battered and broken, squinting in pain and wonder, that Job can confess that he sees God with his own eyes—and for the very first time. Only when the self has been de-centred does fearing God 'for nothing' (i.e. for God's own sake) become a genuine possibility. Once we grasp this, we can begin to understand how even humiliation, loneliness and grief have the potential to deepen our life with God. Painful experiences, which undermine our self-sufficiency and self-centredness, can propel us towards God. This is especially evident at the end of Job's story, where he continues to fear God (i.e. to respond to him as Lord) 'for nothing', free from any sense of entitlement. (We will come back to this in the next chapter.) But there is more to Job's response than his fresh vision of God. As we noted earlier, the word 'therefore' at the beginning of verse 6 suggests that Job's new (in)sight has profound implications for him personally:

> 5 As a report to the ear, I had heard of you,
>   but now my eye sees you.
> 6 Therefore I reject,
>   and change my mind about, 'dust and ashes.' [see 30.19]

The implications of Job's new Theocentric worldview are that he rejects and repents of dust and ashes. But what does this mean?[8] It seems a rather strange thing to say in what is arguably the most important verse in the entire book. Can we identify what is *happening* to Job at this critical juncture in the story?

Only twice in the entire book does the phrase 'dust and ashes' appear; here (42.6) and back in 30.19 at the peak of Job's argument. As I understand the book, this is very significant. In chapter 30, Job expressed disgust with the way his own Maker had treated him: 'He has hurled me into the clay, and I have become like dust and ashes' (30.19). But now, Job retracts his case against God's disorderly management of the world and withdraws the allegation that God is a bully who has dehumanized him. No, it is more than that—Job *rejects* and *repents* of that allegation.

God's freedom from strictly adhering to the rule of karma means neither that he lacks the power and wisdom to manage creation, nor that he has treated Job like dust and ashes. As it turns out, Job's initial response to suffering was right: 'Yahweh gives and Yahweh takes away' (1.21). However, this does not always happen in ways that human beings can anticipate or even comprehend. God gives stupidity and speed to the ostrich and sends rain on a desert for reasons we don't understand—'for nothing,' one might say. But our lack of understanding about God's purposes does not make him a bully. On the contrary, God's profound freedom to give gifts in whatever place and whatever time he chooses is a wondrous, albeit mysterious, aspect of his character. And as Job now appears to understand, human beings may exercise their freedom as God's image-bearers by reflecting this 'for nothing' dimension of God's character. Job's newfound freedom comes to expression in the final verses of the book, but first we must hear the final word in this conversation—God's final word.

Right Speech

In the last three chapters of this book, we have seen how shifts in Job's character are evidenced in his speech: his response when karma fails, his attitude towards the clichéd wisdom of his friends, and his personal engagement with God through questions. As the story draws to a close in chapter 42, Job's speech is highlighted once again when Yahweh turns to Eliphaz and directly addresses the issue of God-talk:

> After Yahweh spoke these words to Job, Yahweh said to Eliphaz the Temanite: 'I am furious with you and with your two friends, since you have not spoken to me rightly, like my servant Job. So now, take seven bulls and seven rams, and go to my servant Job; offer up a burnt-offering for yourselves and my servant Job will pray on your behalf. For if I lift his face,[9] I will refrain from disgracing you; since you have not spoken to me rightly, like my servant Job.' So Eliphaz the Temanite, Bildad the Shuhite and Zophar the Naamathite went and did what Yahweh told them; and Yahweh lifted Job's face (Job 42.7–9).

What does God mean when he says that Job's speech is more 'right' than that of his friends? Is he condoning *all* of Job's speech, or is he only happy with the repentant tone of Job's most recent response (42.1–6)? Surely, if God wanted to affirm only Job's final words, he would have said as much to Job, but it is Eliphaz whom God addresses in verse 7. It would hardly be fair for God to make a comparison between the lengthy speeches of the friends (throughout chapters 3–31) and Job's final few words (in 42.1–6). No, God is comparing the way both Job and his friends have spoken throughout the entire book: 'you have not . . . as my servant Job has.' That is why God instructs the three friends to bring a sacrifice and to ask Job to pray for them; the point is that they have spoken wrongly in the very same context in which Job has spoken rightly.

But in what way has Job's speech about God been 'right'? This divine approval of Job's speech must be the biggest twist in the entire story! Has God witnessed the same speeches we have? With all the accusations Job has directed towards God—of rejecting the righteous while shining on the wicked (10.3); of violently assaulting Job (16.9–14); of acting wrongly (19.6); of being cruel (30.21)—how can God possibly draw the conclusion that Job has spoken 'rightly'? And how is God's verdict to be understood in the light of his opening question from the whirlwind: 'Who is this, casting a shadow over wisdom with ignorant speech?' (Job 38.2). If Job has spoken in ignorance, why does God now proceed to vindicate him before his friends? Or to put a finer point on it, what is commendable about Job's speech if it has not been correct in *content*? The narrative offers up two clues in answer to this question.

a) You have not spoken rightly ...
The Hebrew word (*nekonah*) often translated as 'right' or 'rightly' in verse 7 literally refers to that which is 'fixed' or 'established'.[10] So you could say that Job's speech is praised for reflecting *the way things really are*. While Job's friends may have occasionally got things right,[11] their efforts to uphold human standards of justice by relegating God to a box have incurred God's anger. Only Job, the faithful rebel who speaks his mind before (and even *against*) God, is finally vindicated as the one who speaks rightly. Job has refused to deny any aspect of his experience in order to cling to previous (mis)conceptions of God and justice, as his friends have advised him. Nor has he given up and cursed God, as the Accuser predicted and as his wife recommended. Job may not have spoken with adequate wisdom or sufficient understanding of God's ways, but none can doubt that he has spoken honestly about reality.

b) You have not spoken rightly to me ...
A second clue that explains God's approval of Job's speech is in the particular wording of God's rebuke to Eliphaz: 'you have not spoken rightly *to* me.'[12] That is to say, God is angry with the three friends because they have settled for speaking *about* God instead of addressing him directly. Not once in the entire book do the three friends use the words 'you' or 'yours' of God, though Job often does so—115 times, to be precise.[13] And now, at the story's end, the significance of this detail comes to light. Job has spoken 'rightly' because he has spoken *to* God, and a comment he made earlier suggests that Job has understood the dangers of speaking *for* and *about* God all along. Frustrated with the way his friends insisted on defending God, Job had challenged them:

> Will it go well for you when he examines you?
> ... He will definitely rebuke you
> if you secretly show prejudice (Job 13.9a,10).

In the end, it is just as Job predicted. The friends are rebuked for reaching a foregone conclusion in God's favour, and by contrast, Job is commended for making a concerted effort to engage with God. Even in the latter speech cycles when Job sought third parties to speak on his behalf, he did so because of his desire to engage *with* God, not in order to add fuel to the fire with more theological disputes *about* God.

How then is Job's God-talk 'right'? We may safely surmise that while the *content* of Job's speech (i.e. his specific accusations against God) is wrong now and then, the *mode* of his speech (i.e. its Godward trajectory and raw honesty) is right. Both of the clues in verse 7—'rightly' and 'to me'—suggest that God is pleased with Job for conversing with him as a living, personal Being.

In a creative study of the book of Job, Gerald Janzen shares the story of an argument he had with his daughter one day over whether or not her violin lesson would go ahead as planned. She didn't want to go, but he was adamant:

> Finally, when attempts on both sides to be reasonable had exhausted themselves, I said . . . 'Get your coat and come along; we're going.' At which point, my eleven-year-old daughter sank back in the couch like a cornered mouse, her eyes blazed, and she said with urgent intensity, 'I hate you, Daddy!' Whoa! Wrong course of action! Not on her part; on mine. There was no lesson for her that day; that issue was resolved in other ways. The lesson that day was for me. That my daughter would confront me in that way left me shaken to the core and at the same time profoundly thankful. The 'I hate you!' that belonged to that specific occasion and its issues was grounded in and made possible by a relationship named in the word 'Daddy.'[14]

That stark phrase, 'I hate you, Daddy!' captures both of the elements that are commended in Job's God-talk: direct speech and honest engagement with reality. I was moved by the way Janzen interpreted his daughter's words. What a profound reminder of the way our heavenly Father listens when we address him directly with our hearts laid open.

Dig Deeper

- God answers Job with questions in Job 38—41. Jesus often turns questions back on people in the gospels, too. Why do you think this is?

- Read Matthew 20.1—16. Do you feel that God owes you anything? Explain.

- How can you acknowledge God as 'the True Centre' in your daily life?

- Do you agree with the author when he says that 'painful experiences . . . can propel us towards God'? (p. 70)

- How does this chapter challenge you in your prayer life?

6

The Gospel of Job

> *I had been my whole life a bell, and never knew it
> until at that moment I was lifted and struck.*
> ~ ANNIE DILLARD, Pilgrim at Tinker Creek

Newfound Freedom

Can we really speak of the gospel of Job? The book of Job is rarely described as hopeful or inspiring. It is better known for raising questions about the relationship between God and suffering—and for offering rather limited answers. I suppose some might see good news in the happy ending that eventuates for Job, but more often than not readers are perplexed by verse 10, which seems to reaffirm the certainty of karma after all:

> And so Yahweh restored Job once he had prayed on behalf of his friends; Yahweh multiplied everything Job had owned before, doubling it (Job 42.10).

The restoration of Job's fortunes is often interpreted in one of two ways, neither of which is very satisfying. On one hand, the words 'twice as much' put a furrow in our brow because a 'happily ever after' ending deconstructs what we had thought to be the moral of the story. It's almost as if karma raises its head in triumph just in time to wink as we close the book. *Ha! People get what they deserve, after all!* On the other hand, God's blessings upon Job are sometimes perceived as a return to the beginning, as though Job were being given the opportunity to start over. This is how one of the main characters in Archibald MacLeish's Pulitzer-winning play, *J.B.*, understands the conclusion to Job's story—and he is furious about it! When he is informed that Job 'gets all he ever had and more',[1] he objects angrily:

> Live his life again? —
> Not even the most ignorant, obstinate,
> Stupid or degraded man
> This filthy planet ever farrowed,
> Offered the opportunity to live
> His bodily life twice over, would accept it —
> Least of all Job, poor, trampled bastard![2]

It is fair to ask who would want to 'live his life again' after suffering to such extremes, but this response is based on the understanding that Job's restoration takes him back to where he started, and that is not what happens. The closing epilogue is explicit about Job receiving a double blessing after all his trials, but it also offers some clear indications that karma has not won the day, that Job's tale does not circle back to where it began, and most importantly, that the Accuser was wrong about Job—and God.

First of all, at the beginning of his story Job was characterized as a man who made a habit of praying for his children after their dinner parties, just in case someone sinned in a way that would invite judgement. Those prayers were depicted as being *for something*, namely the security of Job's family. At the story's conclusion, Job is once again in a posture of prayer, but the decisive difference is that Job's prayers are now offered *for nothing*, as a gift.[3] He is no longer praying for personal gain. Although Job is *still* a man of prayer, one who bears others up in his relationship with God, he is not the *same* man of prayer. Praying for his friends, who have brought him nothing but intensified loneliness and narrow-minded judgement (and who never once prayed for him) is an extraordinary act of grace—and the first sign of Job's newfound freedom. In the end, does Job fear God for nothing? Apparently so. And perhaps that is why we hear nothing more from the Accuser.

Fearing God 'for nothing' does not mean, however, that God is unresponsive. God made the point in his response to Job that he is not obligated to behave according to human notions of order and entitlement, but this does not mean that God offers nothing in return for our worship. On the contrary, he is inconceivably generous, beyond our understanding and beyond our very best dreams. The rebuilding of Job's previous relationships is but one expression of this grace in the closing chapter, where the loss of community which he mourned so desperately in chapters 29–30 is restored:

> And all of his brothers and sisters came to him and everyone who had known him previously, and they ate bread with him in his house. They showed him sympathy and comforted him for all the badness that Yahweh had brought upon him. Each of them gave him a certain amount of money and one gold earring (42.11).

Back in chapter 2, Job's friends gathered to offer him 'sympathy and comfort' (2.11), and we have seen how dismally they failed in that task. The same two words now reappear in the epilogue in a more hopeful context. Old friends, bearing gifts, gather around a table of fellowship, and Job receives genuine 'sympathy and comfort' for all that he has endured (42.11). It is difficult to fathom the magnitude of such a moment for Job, whose pain was exacerbated horribly by the misunderstanding of his community. Vindication was not something he had needed for the sake of his pride, but for the preservation of his soul.

A second expression of Job's newfound freedom is the way he breaks free of cultural conventions by treating his daughters as equals with their brothers. Perhaps Job takes his cues from the goats and asses of mountains and salt plains after all, by choosing to live beyond the transactional norms of society. The narrator also chimes in on this point, citing the unorthodox names Job gives his three daughters—Dove, Cinnamon and Mascara[4]—and emphasizing their beauty:

> And he had seven sons and three daughters. He called the first Jemimah, the second Keziah, and the third Keren-happuch. And in all the land no women could be found who were as beautiful as Job's daughters; their father gave them an inheritance along with their brothers (Job 42.13–15).

Actually, given what Job has learned about the world, it is quite remarkable that he has more children at all. Job now knows that neither children themselves nor their safety can be secured through transactions with God. Each child is an undeserved gift born into a broken world, and for the Job we met in chapter 1, this entails a great deal of humility and risk.

Job breaks cultural bonds in another way as well. His possessions and family members were listed in Job 1.2–3 and they are listed again in Job 42.12–13. But while all of the animal numbers are doubled (as we have been led to expect), one element is missing altogether. Do you see it?

And he brought into the world seven sons and three daughters. He owned 7,000 sheep, 3,000 camels, 500 pairs of oxen, 500 donkeys, and also a huge number of servants (Job 1.2–3a).	And he had 14,000 sheep, 6,000 camels, 1,000 yoke of oxen, and 1,000 donkeys. He also had seven sons and three daughters (Job 42.12–13).

In the latter report, Job has no servants. Details like this in Hebrew narrative may be subtle, but they are almost always significant. Perhaps the narrator means to inform readers of yet another way in which Job has decided to break with social conventions. A man of such extravagant wealth with no servants? Now that is as awe-inspiring as the giant sea monster described in Job 41! In the end, as one prominent Jewish scholar has put it, 'Job is a book not so much about God's justice as about the *transformation* of a man.'[5]

Pain + Prayer

No matter how impressed we are with Job's new lease on life in these final verses, most of us are aware that personal tragedy does not automatically lead to positive transformation. Bitterness and resentment are also possible outcomes for those whose lot has been thrown in with the wicked, who unfairly suffer curses instead of blessings. As we conclude our study of Job, therefore, it is important to ask: what is it about *Job's way through pain* that enables him to emerge at the end with newfound freedom? How and why does Job's experience of suffering lead to a hopeful conclusion? To answer these questions, it will be helpful to glance back over the entire story and consider in summary what has happened to Job:

> The entire drama began with a certain mechanical understanding of the world, shared by Job and his friends. But when the story's opening equilibrium is horribly disrupted, Job's belief in **karma** fails to account for his undeserved suffering. Certain that justice has been turned on its head, Job is compelled to seek out the cause and purpose of his afflictions, and his friends are only too willing to help. But their tendency to reduce life's complexities to formulaic **clichés** proves hopelessly inadequate for the task and Job resorts to honest and angry **questions** in his search for a theology that will explain his life crisis. Where karma and clichés fail, questions succeed—at least in providing a means to probe for answers. And so, throughout the cycles of speeches, Job continues to press God with searching questions about the nature of reality: Who can question God? (9.12); Where is hope to be found? (17.15); Why do the wicked prosper? (Job 21.7). Job's many questions eventually open up a **conversation** with God: Job asks one last time why he is getting such a raw deal; God responds by making it clear that he, the True Centre, is not bound by any human notion of entitlement; and Job repents of his accusation that God is a bully who has cruelly turned Job back into dust. Surprisingly, this conversation ends with God affirming Job for being a man of honest prayer. Job's final vindication rests on the rightness of his speech—*to* God about the way things *really* are. After Job prays for his so-called friends, God restores Job's fortunes, granting him double of everything he initially had (although he evidently has the same number of children and no slaves). Having broken free from the strictures of deservedness and entitlement, Job comes to discover that, like his Maker, he can afford to be extravagantly generous and gracious to those around him—even for no apparent reason.

In light of all this, we can say that Job's transformation occurs because his questions, as a means of dealing with pain, open up a conversation with God. Pain alone is not transformative, but Job's determination to understand his traumatic experiences within the context of a relationship with God leads to certain shifts in his character: suffering, endurance, virtue, hope.[6] It is equally important to notice that Job's fresh vision of God ('now my eye sees you') does not come about because he overcomes or moves beyond his pain, but because he insists on conversing with God *within* that agonizing context.

The same dynamic can be seen in the life of the apostle Paul. In a letter to the church in Corinth, Paul shares an experience he had when he was tempted by pride after receiving a special vision:

> . . . because of these surpassingly great revelations . . . in order to keep me from becoming conceited, I was given a thorn in my flesh, a messenger of Satan, to torment me. Three times I pleaded with the Lord to take it away from me. But he said to me, 'My grace is sufficient for you, for my power is made perfect in weakness.' Therefore I will boast all the more gladly about my weaknesses, so that Christ's power may rest on me. That is why, for Christ's sake, I delight in weaknesses, in insults, in hardships, in persecutions, in difficulties. For when I am weak, then I am strong (2 Cor 12.7–10 NIV).

Paul reports that he was 'given' a thorn in his flesh to serve a specific purpose: 'to keep me from becoming conceited'. Perhaps it was a physical form of pain; perhaps it was mental or emotional. In any case, he uses strong language to describe it: 'a messenger of Satan, to torment me.' As one might expect, Paul prayed—three times, no less—for healing or deliverance from this thorn. But God said no. Why? Because the painful thorn brought Paul face to face with the transforming reality of God's grace, permitting him to glimpse an entirely new dimension of this God whose divine power is made perfect in human weakness.

THORNS IN THE FLESH

Paul describes the thorn in his flesh in contradictory terms: it is both a messenger of Satan and the agent of Christ's grace and power. In this way, it is comparable to the unwelcome devastation in Job's life, incited by the satan but used by God to lead Job into newfound freedom.

John draws out a similar dynamic in his gospel; Jesus, in his darkest hour, is beaten like a criminal, wearing a royal robe and a crown of thorns. The crucified King suffers so that you and I, by believing in him, may receive grace and power. This, in turn, becomes the pattern for our lives in Christ:

> We are afflicted in every way, but not crushed; perplexed, but not driven to despair; persecuted, but not forsaken; struck down, but not destroyed; always carrying in the body the death of Jesus, so that the life of Jesus may also be made visible in our bodies. For while we live, we are always being given up to death for Jesus' sake, so that the life of Jesus may be made visible in our mortal flesh (2 Cor 4.8–11 NRSV).

What Paul initially perceived as a handicap enabled him to see something valuable 'in weaknesses, in insults, in hardships, in persecutions, in difficulties.' And if such conditions made more room for Christ's power in Paul's life and ministry, then they were welcome; 'For when I am weak, then I am strong.' *Anything* for the cause of Christ.

Pain paved a way towards the grace of God for Paul just as it did for Job. But the point I wish to make (again) is that Paul's new understanding of strength in weakness did not come about simply because he had a thorn in his side. The critical element in Paul's transformative experience was his insistence on sustaining a conversation with God in the midst of his painful circumstances. Like the book of Job, Paul's testimony in 2 Corinthians 12 centres on a conversation between him and the Lord, and that exchange—Paul's plea for healing and God's tough reply—is what led to a radical shift in Paul's life and ministry.[7]

The practical implications of all this are quite clear: we can't afford to stop communicating with God when life treats us unfairly. If our experiences of pain and injustice are to be transformative, then we *must not* give up on prayer—even when, like Job, we begin to wonder whether anyone is really listening. What's more, as the book of Job suggests, there are no guarantees that God will ever answer as we hope or expect. God's answer from the whirlwind is neither logical nor reassuring; rather, God de-centres Job and makes him feel small. In answer to Paul's plea that the thorn in his flesh be removed, God answers 'No'. To Jesus' prayer in the garden of Gethsemane—'let this cup pass from me'[8]—God answers 'No'.

In my own life, I have lived with an unanswered prayer concerning a severely unjust set of circumstances for almost ten years now. Without going into detail, I can honestly say that learning to live and pray with the ongoing repercussions of another person's malice has given me a deeper appreciation for God's grace. Perhaps a better way of putting it is that I have begun to understand the positive value of affliction. By God's grace, I am more able to empathize with others and restrain judgement because of my own journey (2 Cor 1.4), and from time to time I find myself bearing witness to an inner strength that is certainly not my own (2 Cor 4.7). When close friends ask how I have been so resilient, the truest answer I can give is that God's grace and power reach their full strength in human need and weakness (2 Cor 12.9). As I said at the close of the first chapter, you may never find a satisfactory, logical explanation for the suffering or injustice you are enduring. But if you persist in his presence, the personal transformation that results from your encounter with the living God will undoubtedly be a better 'answer' than the one you went looking for.

This certainly appears to have been true for Job. As the whirlwind subsides and the dust settles, Job steps out with a new sense of purpose and identity. Not only is his belief in a transactional god overcome by a fresh glimpse of Yahweh as the True Centre, but Job's compulsive, religious habit described at the beginning of his story also gives way to gratuitous actions that reflect the likeness of his Creator. Such transformation is the consequence not of pain alone, but of pain + prayer.

All of this is well and good, but I do not doubt that some readers still wonder why Christians are not shielded from pain altogether. Isn't there a way that God can shape us into his image through prayer and positive experiences, leaving pain out of the equation? Without promising any easy answers, I wish to address this question briefly by identifying how God sometimes uses pain to help us navigate the divide between karma (deserved blessing) and grace (undeserved blessing).

From Karma to Grace

At the end of chapter two, I affirmed that the notion of karma has some merit and should not be dismissed altogether (provided God is understood to be the One who administers justice). I stress this again here because Christians have a tendency to think that justice gets traded in for grace when we turn the page from Malachi to Matthew. The truth, however, is that both justice *and* grace are affirmed in both the Old *and* New Testaments.[9] The message of the book of Job, for its part, does not deny God's justice; but it stresses that God is free to order and judge the world according to his inscrutable wisdom. For Christians today living under the new covenant, grace and justice are both indispensable and are best understood in relation to one another.

On its own, a strict theology of just desserts functions like an anti-gospel in the life of the believer, driving us to strive more, do more, achieve more—so that we deserve more. Karma not only asserts that we deserve to reap *everything* that we have sown, but it stipulates that we deserve to reap *only* what we have sown. By itself, karma leaves no room for grace; you get *exactly* what you deserve.

Grace, on the other hand, is *un*deserved blessing, a free gift. The staggering claim of the gospel is that 'while we were still sinners Christ died for us' (Rom 5.8 NRSV). Not after you confessed your need of forgiveness; not after you cleaned up your act; not even because you promised to serve God with your life. No, it was while you were oblivious to your need of God, perhaps even actively resistant to him, that Jesus died for you. And whether or not you feel that you deserve such a gift makes absolutely no difference to the fact that it has already been accomplished. Jesus' saving death for you is a free gift, and there will *never* be *anything* you can do to deserve it. God's grace for you in Jesus Christ is the heart and soul of the gospel.

Even so, most of us are at least intuitively aware that we gravitate towards karma rather than grace, no matter how long we've been Christians. We know the biblical teaching: that forgiveness and fullness of life are ours simply on account of believing in the saving death and resurrection of Jesus. But trusting that our own salvation is entirely outside of our control is an enormous act of surrender. We would rather fulfil a long list of musts and shoulds. Why? Because receiving such an extravagant gift devastates our self-sufficiency and pride. To put it quite simply, we want to deserve the things we have. And so, for the sake of our pride we quietly and subtly resist the amazing gospel of grace and opt instead for trying to make ourselves worthy of salvation. Even if this message of grace was received with gratitude in the first instance, as time passes many Christians fall into the habit of striving to demonstrate to God and to themselves that they actually deserve it.[10] Of course, it is somewhat ironic that we strive to earn something that was freely given to us, but at the end of the day (and of our lives) we want—or perhaps need—to feel that we deserve, or have earned, the saving of our souls. The problem is, this insistence on having what we deserve not only holds God's transformative grace at bay; it also feeds our pride by strengthening our sense of entitlement.

I suspect this is part of the reason Paul received a negative answer when he asked God to remove the thorn from his flesh. The Lord, in his wisdom, chose not to restore Paul's self-sufficiency by making him whole again. Instead of replacing sickness with health or difficulty with ease, God gave Paul the grace to bear with his affliction so that his situation could be completely changed even without the removal of the thorn. What transformed Paul and his painful situation was the humble recognition that *God's glory shines through human frailty.* Thus Paul could even say in hindsight that he was 'given' the thorn to prevent him from becoming 'conceited' (NIV), or more literally, from 'exalting himself'.

I remember having a conversation with my mother some years ago as I was trying to come to terms with the situation I mentioned earlier. She told me she could see that a change was being wrought in me as a result of the difficulties I was experiencing. When I asked her what she meant, she replied, 'Suffering humbles you.' Time slowed as those words sank in. If anyone could speak with authority on such matters, my mother could. (By that time, her arthritis had her bound to a wheelchair.) She was right; pain is humbling, and with it comes an opportunity to move from a sense of entitlement towards grace.

This does not mean that every person in pain is, by implication, someone God wishes to humble. The difficult circumstances of Jamie, Roslyn and Wesley from the opening chapter are not evidence of their need for more humility. Making that kind of assumption returns us to the error of Job's friends, who seek a formula for everything that happens in life. To label all sufferers as 'sinful' or 'proud' is to learn absolutely nothing from the book of Job. A painful experience may very well be used by God to facilitate a movement towards grace in our lives, but we cannot speak with certainty about the cause and purpose of every such event. Also, there is a world of difference between saying, 'God caused this painful event to happen in order to teach me something' and 'God is working redemptively within this situation, even though it surely grieves him as much as it hurts me.' The reality of living in a broken world[11] is that suffering will inevitably intrude on our lives in some way or another, whether through injustice, physical or mental inability, addiction, loss, estrangement, or something else. And when it does, we may hope and trust that our painful circumstances, however unwelcome, will permit a greater openness to Christ's power and presence.

Also, we mustn't forget that this pain-induced move towards grace in the lives of Job and Paul is only an indicator, the outworking, of an even more profound reality: the very God of gift and grace to whom they bear witness has willingly submitted himself to pain and injustice for our sakes. Instead of crowning himself king, Jesus chose to identify with us by 'being born in human likeness' (Phil 2.7 NRSV). As a fully human being, God suffered with us and for us, enduring the very worst kinds of pain: horrific violence coupled with godforsakenness. Falsely accused by his own people, Jesus was brutally beaten and nailed to a cross by Roman soldiers. And upon that cross where he was left to die, his final prayer—a heart-wrenching question—was left unanswered: 'My God, my God, why have you forsaken me?'

Despite how strange all of this sounds to those of us who would do almost anything to rise above our painful circumstances, Paul calls Jesus the 'power of God and the wisdom of God' (1 Cor 1.24 NRSV). In God's otherworldly wisdom, he loves us, shapes us, and draws near to us *in and through suffering*. And this is not just a theological claim, written down in an ancient document for us to read about; this radical truth has been made known to us in the flesh and blood of Jesus, who did not redeem the world by rising above its problems, but by immersing himself in them. *God with us* in our pain. As the prophet Isaiah marvelled, *Behold, this is our God!*[12]

As we conclude this study of *Job's way through pain*, there is still the matter of your questions. You may have an interest in the book of Job as literature, you may have tough questions arising from your own experiences, or perhaps you are looking for something else altogether. But the implications of Job's story rest now with you. Perhaps you will pray differently, hope differently, speak differently to others who are hurting. Whatever your life context, I trust and pray that the transformation that occurred in Job's life as a result of his pain—from an insistence on entitlement to an engagement with the living God of grace—will occur in your life as well.

May it be so.

Dig Deeper

- In what ways is Job different at the end of the book from how he was at the beginning?

- How can you reflect the extravagant generosity of God?

- In what way(s) can a 'thorn in the flesh' lead to positive transformation in the life of a believer?

- How do you 'gravitate towards karma rather than grace' (p. 84)?

- What 'good news' have you discovered in the book of Job?

You are invited to continue exploring the Bible with Paul Hedley Jones at **textofmeeting.com**

The Tent of Meeting was the designated place for Moses and the people of Israel to meet with God as they traveled through the desert (Exod 33.7f.). It was God's portable dwelling place, enabling him to remain close to his people as they made their spiritual and physical journey from slavery in Egypt to freedom in the Promised Land. John picks up on this image in the New Testament by introducing Jesus as God's revelatory Word who 'tabernacled' among us (Jn. 1.14) so that God might fully be made known to humanity. Jesus is, as John puts it, the enfleshed Word of God.

The Bible has served a similar purpose to the Tent of Meeting for centuries now, as the *Text* of Meeting for God's people, presenting opportunities for us to encounter him regularly as we discern the way. **textofmeeting.com** is an online space, devoted to enabling fellow pilgrims to learn more about this special text through which God desires to meet with us.

Bibliography

Balentine, Samuel E. *Job* (Macon, GA: Smyth & Helwys, 2006).
Bonhoeffer, Dietrich. *Letters and Papers from Prison: An Abridged Edition* (Norwich: SCM Press, 2001).
Brown, William P. *Character in Crisis: A Fresh Approach to the Wisdom Literature of the Old Testament* (Grand Rapids: Eerdmans, 1996).
Brueggemann, Walter. *The Covenanted Self: Explorations in Law and Covenant* (Minneapolis: Fortress Press, 1999).
— *Old Testament Theology: Essays on Structure, Theme and Text* (Minneapolis: Fortress Press, 1992).
— 'A Response to Professor Childs'. *Scottish Journal of Theology* 53/2 (2000): pp. 234–8.
— *Theology of the Old Testament: Testimony, Dispute, Advocacy* (Minneapolis: Fortress Press, 1997).
Buechner, Frederick. *The Magnificent Defeat* (New York: Seabury Press, 1966).
Chapman, Stephen B. *The Law and the Prophets: A Study in Old Testament Canon Formation*. Forschungen zum Alten Testament 27 (Tübingen: Mohr Siebeck, 2000).
Childs, Brevard S. *Old Testament Theology in a Canonical Context* (Philadelphia: Fortress Press, 1985).
Davis, Ellen F. *Getting Involved with God: Rediscovering the Old Testament* (Cambridge: Cowley, 2001).
Didion, Joan. *The Year of Magical Thinking* (New York: Knopf, 2005).
Ford, David F. *Christian Wisdom: Desiring God and Learning in Love* (Cambridge: Cambridge University Press, 2007).
Fretheim, Terence E. *Creation Untamed: The Bible, God and Natural Disasters* (Grand Rapids: Baker Academic, 2010).
Goldingay, John. *Job for Everyone* (Louisville, KY: Westminster John Knox Press, 2013).
Goldman, William. *The Princess Bride: S. Morgenstern's Classic Tale of True Love and High Adventure* (Boston: Houghton Mifflin Harcourt, abridged edn, 2013).

Good, Edwin M. *In Turns of Tempest: A Reading of Job, with a Translation* (Stanford: Stanford University Press, 1990).

Greenberg, Moshe. *Studies in the Bible and Jewish Thought* (Philadelphia: Jewish Publication Society, 1995).

Habel, Norman C. *The Book of Job* (Cambridge: Cambridge University Press, 1975).

Hill, Wesley. *Washed and Waiting: Reflections on Christian Faithfulness and Homosexuality* (Grand Rapids: Zondervan, 2010).

Hugo, Victor. *Les Misérables* (trans. Julie Rose; London: Vintage, 2008 [orig. 1862]).

Janzen, Gerald. *At the Scent of Water: The Ground of Hope in the Book of Job* (Grand Rapids: Eerdmans, 2009).

Jones, Paul Hedley. *Sharing God's Passion: Prophetic Spirituality* (Milton Keynes: Paternoster Press, 2012).

Kafka, Franz. *The Trial* (orig. trans. Willa and Edwin Muir; rev. trans. E.M. Butler; New York: Schocken, 1995).

Kelemen, Deborah. 'Are Children "Intuitive Theists"? Reasoning about Purpose and Design in Nature'. *Psychological Science* 15/5 (2004): pp. 295–301.

Koch, Klaus. 'Is There a Doctrine of Retribution in the Old Testament?' Pages 57–87 in *Theodicy in the Old Testament. Issues in Religion and Theology* 4 (ed. James L. Crenshaw; Philadelphia: Fortress Press; London: SPCK, 1983).

Levenson, Jon D. *Creation and the Persistence of Evil: The Jewish Drama of Divine Omnipotence* (Princeton: Princeton University Press, 1988).

Lewis, C.S. *A Grief Observed* (London: Faber & Faber, 1961).

Longman III, Tremper. *Job* (Grand Rapids: Baker Academic, 2012).

MacLeish, Archibald. *J.B.* (Boston: Houghton Mifflin, 1956).

Martel, Yann. *Life of Pi* (Edinburgh, Canongate, 2001).

Moberly, R.W.L. *The Bible, Theology and Faith: A Study of Abraham and Jesus* (Cambridge: Cambridge University Press, 2000).

Newsom, Carol. *The Book of Job*. New Interpreter's Bible, vol. 4 (Nashville: Abingdon Press, 1996), pp. 319–637.

Patrick, Dale. 'Job's Address of God'. *Zeitschrift für die Alttestamentliche Wissenschaft* 91 (1979): pp. 268–82.

Piaget, Jean. *The Moral Judgment of the Child* (trans. Marjorie Gabain; New York: Harcourt, 1932).

Plantinga Jr, Cornelius. *Not the Way It's Supposed to Be: A Breviary of Sin* (Grand Rapids: Eerdmans, 1995).

Sorrentino, Richard and Yamaguchi, Susumu, eds. *Handbook of Motivation and Cognition across Cultures* (London: Elsevier, 2008).

Sternberg, Meir. *The Poetics of Biblical Narrative: Ideological Literature and the Drama of Reading* (Bloomington: Indiana University Press, 1985).

Ticciati, Susannah. *Job and the Disruption of Identity: Reading beyond Barth* (London: T&T Clark, 2005).

von Rad, Gerhard. *Wisdom in Israel* (trans. James D. Martin; Harrisburg, PA: Trinity Press International, 1972 [orig. 1970]).

Weber, Max. *The Religion of India: The Sociology of Hinduism and Buddhism* (New York: Free Press, 1958).

Wiesel, Elie. *The Trial of God (as it was held on February 25, 1649, in Shamgorod)* (New York: Schocken, 1979).

Wolfers, David. *Deep Things out of Darkness: The Book of Job, Essays and a New English Translation* (Grand Rapids: Eerdmans, 1995).

Wolterstorff, Nicolas. *Lament for a Son* (Grand Rapids: Eerdmans, 1987).

Endnotes

1. SETTING THE SCENE

[1] In the book, it is Fezzik's mother who says these words; in the film adaptation, it is Westley. William Goldman, *The Princess Bride: S. Morgenstern's Classic Tale of True Love and High Adventure* (Boston: Houghton Mifflin Harcourt, abridged edn, 2013), p. 161.

[2] Joan Didion, *The Year of Magical Thinking* (New York: Knopf, 2005), p. 3 (original emphasis).

[3] Wesley's first book, a theological memoir about being faithful to Christ as a homosexual, is entitled *Washed and Waiting: Reflections on Christian Faithfulness and Homosexuality* (Grand Rapids: Zondervan, 2010).

[4] See Rom 8.24–25.

[5] Dietrich Bonhoeffer, *Letters and Papers from Prison: An Abridged Edition* (Norwich: SCM Press, 2001), p. 40.

[6] For more information about why *Satan* as a proper name is a 'misleading translation', see John Goldingay, *Job for Everyone* (Louisville, KY: Westminster John Knox, 2013), pp. 12–13.

[7] Tremper Longman III, *Job* (Grand Rapids: Baker Academic, 2012), p. 92.

[8] See Samuel Balentine's commentary *Job* (Macon, GA: 2006), in the Smyth & Helwys series, which includes photographic reproductions of artwork inspired by the book of Job as well as numerous references to other related works.

2. KARMA

[1] Max Weber, *The Religion of India: The Sociology of Hinduism and Buddhism* (New York: Free Press, 1958), p. 121.

[2] Jean Piaget, *The Moral Judgment of the Child* (trans. Marjorie Gabain; New York: Harcourt, 1932), p. 250.

[3] For further reading on this, see Deborah Kelemen, 'Are Children "Intuitive Theists"? Reasoning about Purpose and Design in Nature', *PS* 15/5 (2004): pp. 295–301.

[4] Cited in Eric Luis Uhlmann et al., 'Implicit Theism', in *Handbook of Motivation and Cognition across Cultures* (ed. Richard Sorrentino and Susumu Yamaguchi; London: Elsevier, 2008), p. 80.

[5] Gerhard von Rad, *Wisdom in Israel* (trans. James D. Martin; Harrisburg, PA: Trinity, 1972 [orig. 1970]), p. 218.

[6] Genesis 1 also begins with a word-pair that highlights the chapter's subject matter. After the earth is described as 'formless and empty' in Gen 1.2 (NIV), God proceeds to *form* the earth on days 1–3 and *fill* it on days 4–6.

[7] This footnote has little bearing on what I am saying at this point, but I want to alert the reader to an interesting reading of the book of Job. David Wolfers was a medical doctor who quit his practice to spend the last twenty years of his life studying the book of Job, and he understands the parallels between Job and Deut 28 in this way: 'Job's trials must be interpreted as the fulfillment of the curses in the Covenant between God and Israel. For this to be the case Job must be a figure representative of the people of Israel, and the events of the Prologue an allegorical representation of national events affecting the people . . . Looked at as a probable political allegory, the Prologue to Job immediately comes alive with allusions and possibilities. Job's children become the Ten Tribes of Israel (seven sons in cis-Jordan, three daughters in trans-Jordan) obliterated by that *great gale from beyond the desert* (what a telling expression!), Assyria, their final demise taking place in *the House of their first-born brother*, Samaria in the territory of Ephraim. Job and his wife then represent the surviving kingdom of Judah with the tribe of Benjamin' (pp. 116–17). Wolfers goes on to account for many of the obscure details in the opening scenes. He does not claim novelty in his interpretation, but refers readers to the Kabbalist Solomon Molch (ad 1500–32) and to the Midrash of *Exodus Rabbah* (ch. 26; ad 900–1000). David Wolfers, *Deep Things out of Darkness: The Book of Job, Essays and a New English Translation* (Grand Rapids: Eerdmans, 1995), pp. 111–18.

[8] Franz Kafka, *The Trial* (orig. trans. Willa and Edwin Muir; rev. trans. E.M. Butler (New York: Schocken, 1995), p. 3.

⁹ R.W.L. Moberly, *The Bible, Theology, and Faith: A Study of Abraham and Jesus* (Cambridge: CUP, 2000), p. 79.

¹⁰ For instance, Norman Habel opens his 1975 commentary with these words: 'There are two different Jobs in this book, the patient Job and the angry Job.' *The Book of Job* (Cambridge: CUP, 1975), p. 1.

¹¹ Exod 34.7; Num 14.18; Nah 1.3 (NIV).

¹² In 1955, a German scholar named Klaus Koch proposed that some texts in the Old Testament (e.g. Ps 7.15–16) speak of a connection between *deed* and *consequence* without identifying God as the One who enforces reward or punishment. Koch argued that every action creates a 'fate-inducing sphere' around the one performing the action. Thus, good behaviour brings blessing and wholeness while evil actions bring about destruction. (The consequences of David's adultery with Bathsheba are a good example of this.) In some ways, there is very little difference between Koch's 'fate-inducing sphere' and pop culture's concept of karma. Koch's idea has not been very well received in academic circles (mainly because God's agency is reduced to ensuring that natural forces do their work), but his readings of OT texts say something significant about God's ordering of creation. Klaus Koch, 'Is There a Doctrine of Retribution in the Old Testament?', in *Theodicy in the Old Testament*. Issues in Religion and Theology 4 (ed. James L. Crenshaw; Philadelphia: Fortress; London: SPCK, 1983), pp. 57–87.

¹³ Christians recognize that the world is not as it should be, even in spite of God's unlimited power and sovereignty. What I am calling the 'messiness of reality' is, as you can imagine, a big theological question and one that we don't have space to explore in detail here. One possibility is that God created a dynamic world; Terence Fretheim presents the view that God created a 'good' but not 'perfect' world, and that 'the continuing creation of the world' necessarily involves things like natural disasters. See his *Creation Untamed: The Bible, God, and Natural Disasters* (Grand Rapids: Baker Academic, 2010). Another view, presented by Cornelius Plantinga Jr, is that the parasitic presence of sin in the world distorts and violates the way things ought to be. See his *Not the Way It's Supposed to Be: A Breviary of Sin* (Grand Rapids: Eerdmans, 1995). Both books are well worth reading.

3. CLICHÉS

1. Nicolas Wolterstorff, *Lament for a Son* (Grand Rapids: Eerdmans, 1987), p. 34.
2. See ch. 2, n. 13.
3. David F. Ford, *Christian Wisdom: Desiring God and Learning in Love* (Cambridge: CUP, 2007), p. 102.
4. When read together, the quandary is not 'Should I answer the fool or not?' but rather, 'What is the best way to respond in this situation so that (a) I don't end up sounding like a fool myself (as verse 4 recommends) and so that (b) this fool's lack of wisdom is exposed (as verse 5 suggests)?'
5. Victor Hugo, *Les Misérables* (trans. Julie Rose; London: Vintage, 2008 [orig. 1862]), p. 144.
6. Hugo, *Les Misérables*, p. 1081.
7. Hugo, *Les Misérables*, p. 1082.
8. In the novel, however, before ending his life, Javert returns to the police station and requests in writing that a number of laws be changed to ensure more humane treatment of prisoners. Hugo, *Les Misérables*, pp. 1086–7.
9. E.g. Lev 24.19–20; Prov 14.14; Ezek 18 in the OT and 2 Cor 5.10; 2 Thess 1.6–8; Rev 20.13 in the NT. (I am hesitant to simply list references like this; remember always to interpret verses within their contexts!)
10. Rom 15.33, 16.20; Php 4.9; 1 Thess 5.23.
11. The parade example is 2 Sam 24.1 and 1 Chron 21.1.
12. Again, a common example is Jesus' clearing of the temple, which is recorded at the end of the Synoptics (Matthew, Mark and Luke) but at the beginning of John's gospel.
13. The following metaphor is drawn from Walter Brueggemann, *Theology of the Old Testament: Testimony, Dispute, Advocacy* (Minneapolis: Fortress, 1997).
14. Pss 3–7; 10–14; 16–17; 22–23; 25–28; 31; 35–36; 38–43; 51–59; 61–64; 69–71; 73–74; 83; 86; 88; 102; 109; 123; 130; 137; 140–143.
15. Jer 11.18–23; 12.1–6; 15.10–21; 17.14–18; 18.18–23; 20.7–18. The exact references for Jeremiah's confessions vary slightly between interpreters.
16. Brueggemann discusses two additional kinds of testimony as well: *unsolicited* testimony (the human person, the nations and creation) and *embodied* testimony (various mediators including divine presence,

Torah, king, prophet and sage). Brueggemann, *Theology of the Old Testament*, pp. 117–20.

[17] Brueggemann, 'A Response to Professor Childs', *Scottish Journal of Theology* 53/2 (2000): pp. 237.

[18] Scholars often refer to these eight books (Deuteronomy, Joshua, Judges, Ruth, 1–2 Samuel, 1–2 Kings) as the 'Deuteronomistic History' because the theological themes in Deuteronomy give shape and focus to the entire history that follows. Another way of putting it is that all of these books have the same 'Deuteronomistic' flavour.

[19] Paul uses the same phrase—'you reap whatever you sow'—in Gal 6.7, though in a different context.

[20] Also see Eccl 7.15.

[21] E.g., compare Jer 20.14–18 with Job 3.

[22] Yann Martel, *Life of Pi* (Edinburgh: Canongate, 2001), p. 292.

[23] Martel, *Life of Pi*, p. 317.

[24] The interview, conducted by Jennie Renton in 2005, may be read/heard at http://textualities.net/jennie-renton/yann-martel-interview/.

[25] As one very influential scholar has put it, 'Old Testament theology is a continuing enterprise in which each new generation must engage.' Brevard S. Childs, *Old Testament Theology in a Canonical Context* (Philadelphia: Fortress, 1985), p. 12.

[26] Stephen B. Chapman, *The Law and the Prophets: A Study in Old Testament Canon Formation*. Forschungen zum Alten Testament 27 (Tübingen: Mohr Siebeck, 2000), p. 109 (original emphasis).

4. QUESTIONS

[1] *Messiah* comes from the Hebrew word for 'anointed one'. At that point in history, God chose the Persian King Cyrus to deliver Israel. See Isa 45.1.

[2] Incidentally, Isaiah's prophecy addresses Job's question about whether bad things [*ra'*] can come from a good God (Job 2.10)—and he puts the matter quite bluntly:
I form the light and create darkness,
I bring prosperity and create disaster [ra'];
I, the Lord, do all these things (Isa 45.7 NIV).

[3] *Hashem* means 'the Name' (see Lev 24.11). It is how Jews speak of God in conversation, since the name of God itself is considered too holy to utter. In Jewish prayer, however, God's name is pronounced *Adonai*, which means 'Lord'.

4 Walter Brueggemann often makes use of these terms. See, for instance, *The Covenanted Self: Explorations in Law and Covenant* (Minneapolis: Fortress, 1999), pp. 18–34.
5 Walter Brueggemann, *Old Testament Theology: Essays on Structure, Theme and Text* (Minneapolis: Fortress, 1992), p. 28.
6 For an excellent sermon/reflection on this text, see Frederick Buechner, *The Magnificent Defeat* (New York: Seabury, 1966), pp. 10–18.
7 Ellen F. Davis, *Getting Involved With God: Rediscovering the Old Testament* (Cambridge: Cowley, 2001), p. 133.
8 As well as much scholarly work on the legal metaphor in Job, various plays and novels have been written as reflections on this theme. For instance, Elie Wiesel's play, entitled *The Trial of God*, recounts conversations leading to a trial in which God is prosecuted for his lack of intervention in a recent pogrom (an organized massacre of Jews). The full title is *The Trial of God (as it was held on February 25, 1649, in Shamgorod)* (New York: Schocken, 1979).
9 I have charted each occurrence of direct address (darker column) as well as the number of verses containing 'you' (lighter column), since a single verse often contains two or more verbs and pronouns in the second person. Also see the charts in Dale Patrick, 'Job's Address of God', *Zeitschrift für die Alttestamentliche Wissenschaft* 91 (1979): pp. 270–71.
10 Carol A. Newsom, *The Book of Job*, New Interpreter's Bible, vol. 4 (Nashville: Abingdon, 1996), p. 398.
11 The word for 'storm' used in 9.17 ('he would buffet me with a storm' [$s^{e'}arah$]) is also used in Job 38.1 when Yahweh answers Job 'from the storm [$s^{e'}arah$]'.
12 C.S. Lewis, *A Grief Observed* (London: Faber & Faber, 1961), p. 7. Lewis revisits this image of a locked door throughout his journal. In a later entry, he adds, 'I have gradually been coming to feel that the door is no longer shut and bolted. Was it my own frantic need that slammed it in my face? The time when there is nothing at all in your soul except a cry for help may be just the time when God can't give it: you are like the drowning man who can't be helped because he clutches and grabs. Perhaps your own reiterated cries deafen you to the voice you hoped to hear' (p. 40). Still later, he writes, 'Turned to God, my mind no longer meets that locked door . . . There was no sudden, striking, and emotional transition. Like the warming of a room or the coming of daylight. When you first notice them, they have already been going

on for some time' (p. 52). And finally, 'When I lay these questions before God, I get no answer. But a rather special sort of "No answer". It is not the locked door. It is more like a silent, certainly not uncompassionate, gaze. As though he shook his head not in refusal but waiving the question. Like, "Peace, child; you don't understand"' (p. 58).

[13] Job makes the same point in 9.22.

[14] Meir Sternberg, *The Poetics of Biblical Narrative: Ideological Literature and the Drama of Reading* (Bloomington: Indiana University Press, 1985), p. 346.

[15] Or, 'they do not hold back from spitting in my face' (see NIV).

[16] Within the second speech cycle, only 16.7b–8 and 17.3–4 contain second person speech directed to God, and both outbursts share a common subject: Job's rejection from his community because the law of karma has been applied to him.

[17] Verse 18 is notoriously difficult to translate. Edwin Good, with refreshing honesty, leaves most of the verse blank in his commentary and simply states, 'The most I can make of this couplet is an image of clothing' (*In Turns of Tempest: A Reading of Job, with a Translation* [Stanford: Stanford University Press, 1990], pp. 130–31); but see his comments on pp. 184–6 about not wanting to 'rewrite' the Hebrew text). As I understand it, what is imagined here is that God disguises himself in garments familiar to Job in order to catch him out unexpectedly—and violently.

[18] See p. 54.

5. CONVERSATION

[1] God uses penetrating questions to reorient his prophets on occasion, too; e.g. Elijah in 1 Kgs 19.9,13, and Jonah in Jnh 4.4,9. Both of these stories receive a fuller treatment in my book on the spirituality of the prophets, *Sharing God's Passion: Prophetic Spirituality* (Milton Keynes: Paternoster, 2012). On the prophetic task of reorientation and the way it is borne out in Samuel's ministry, see ch. 4 of the same book.

[2] See Job 38.39–39.30; 40.15–41.34.

[3] Stephen B. Chapman, 'God of Nations', chapel sermon at Duke Divinity School, delivered 8 December 2008.

[4] They are not strictly quotations (see p. 63), but the referents, indicated in the square brackets, are obvious enough.

[5] I have borrowed this phrase from Susannah Ticciati, *Job and the Disruption of Identity: Reading beyond Barth* (London: T&T Clark, 2005).

[6] Incidentally, Copernicus himself was both a scientist and a theologian. He worked as canon of a cathedral in Poland from 1506 until his death, and he was well aware that a heliocentric model for the universe was not only contrary to popular philosophical and scientific reasoning, but also considered contrary to the Scriptures. So it wasn't until decades after his discovery that Copernicus finally, at the behest of some students, published his findings. Even then, he presented them only as a tentative theory. He allegedly received a copy of his book on the day of his death (24 May 1543), but it was not until much later that Galileo and Kepler were bold enough to publicly confirm his proposals.

[7] Jon D. Levenson, *Creation and the Persistence of Evil: The Jewish Drama of Divine Omnipotence* (Princeton: Princeton University Press, 1988), pp. 155–6.

[8] I am somewhat reluctant to criticize Bible translations, but I feel it necessary to mention that the most widely accepted translations of 42.6 are distinctly unhelpful. (The only consensus among Hebrew scholars concerning 42.6 is the widespread agreement concerning its mistranslation.) Both the NIV and NRSV translate Job 42.6 as follows: 'therefore I despise myself, and repent in dust and ashes.' However, other translations are possible—and indeed, more grammatically correct. Of course, every translation is an interpretation to some extent, but in some cases a translator's interpretive judgements reduce, or entirely close off, legitimate interpretive possibilities for the reader. (Translation and interpretation should be kept distinct from one another where possible.)

The arguments for translation have been set out in a variety of commentaries and articles, and there is no need for me to repeat them here. See especially Carol Newsom, *Job*, New Interpreter's Bible, vol. 4 (1996), pp. 628–9 and the references in footnotes 606–17. Two brief comments will suffice here: (a) The first verb in 42.6, meaning 'reject' [*ma'as*] never occurs in the Old Testament as a reflexive verb (i.e. I despise myself). As a transitive verb, it requires an object (which translations often provide), but since none follows the verb in the Hebrew text, it is logical to understand 'dust and ashes' as the object of both verbs; (b) The second verb + preposition [*niham-al*] always means to 'repent *of*' and never to 'repent *upon*' or 'repent *in*' (i.e. with a spatial reference) in the Old Testament (see Jer 18.8,10). The NRSV and NIV go against the grammar with regards to both (a) and (b). I propose the following translation:

Therefore I reject,
and change my mind about, 'dust and ashes.'

This translation is based on a straightforward understanding of the Hebrew without providing extra English words for clarity and without performing grammatical gymnastics. However, it does raise an important interpretive question, namely, 'What does it mean to repent of dust and ashes?' There are three possibilities: (a) 'dust and ashes' refers to Job's state of mourning; (b) 'dust and ashes' refers to Job's fragile human condition; (c) 'dust and ashes' refers to the punchline of Job's final speech in 30.19; i.e. that God, a bully of cosmic proportions, has unmade Job and scattered him like 'dust and ashes.' In my judgement, it means very little for Job to repent of (a) his state of mourning or (b) his frail humanity when he has just spent the preceding thirty chapters vehemently arguing his case before God. When one reads the book of Job as a unified story, (c)—Job's accusation against God in 30.19—seems the most sensible referent for 'dust and ashes' in 42.6.

9 The Hebrew idiom 'to lift one's face' has various meanings, depending on its context. Here, as in Gen 19.21 and 1 Sam 25.35, where one person lifts the face of another, the idiom denotes a positive response to a request. Thus, to lift Job's face in this context is for God to favour him by accepting his prayers.

10 The same word occurs in Psalm 5.9 in the context of human speech, suggesting that $n^e konah$ also indicates honesty and truthfulness.

11 For instance, the friends talk about 'the incomprehensibility of the divine activity in creation.' E.g. Job 11.7–9; 36.22–30; 37.2–16. Gerhard von Rad, *Wisdom in Israel* (trans. James D. Martin; Harrisburg, PA: Trinity, 1972 [orig. 1970]), p. 225, n. 47.

12 Most translations say, 'you have not spoken rightly *of* me' as the reason for God's disapproval of the friends, but the grammatical construction used in this verse always means speak *to* rather than speak *of*. According to Janzen, 'of the 150 occurrences of this verb followed by this preposition and a personal pronoun, in 149 instances, the preposition means "to."' Gerald Janzen, *At the Scent of Water: The Ground of Hope in the Book of Job* (Grand Rapids: Eerdmans, 2009), p. 106.

[13] Job 7.7–21; 9.28–31; 10.2–22; 13.20–14.22; 16.7b–8; 17.3–4; 30.20–23; 40.4–5; 42.2–6. See the table on p. 53.
[14] Janzen, *Scent of Water*, p. 93.

6. THE GOSPEL OF JOB

[1] Archibald MacLeish, *J.B.* (Boston: Houghton Mifflin, 1956), p. 142.
[2] MacLeish, *J.B.*, pp. 143–4.
[3] The Septuagint (the primary Greek translation of the Old Testament) translates the Hebrew word *hinnam* ('for nothing') in Job 1.9 using the word *dorean*, meaning 'as a gift'. The sense of the Accuser's question in the Septuagint is, 'Surely Job does not worship God as a gift?' Like many other interpreters, I consider the question in Job 1.9 to be central to the book's meaning.
[4] The third name, *Keren-Happuch* literally means 'horn-of-*happuch*', *happuch* being a black mineral powder like antimony or kohl, used in the ancient world to decorate one's eyes and eyelashes. 'Sensuous names are not the biblical norm, and naming a daughter for a cosmetic is way over the top,' says Ellen F. Davis, *Getting Involved with God: Rediscovering the Old Testament* (Cambridge: Cowley, 2001), p. 142.
[5] Moshe Greenberg, *Studies in the Bible and Jewish Thought* (JPS: Philadelphia, 1995), p. 327, emphasis original.
[6] This progression comes from Rom 5.3–4. For an insightful reading of Job that focuses on character formation, see William P. Brown, 'The Deformation of Character: Job 1–31' and 'The Reformation of Character: Job 32–42', in *Character in Crisis: A Fresh Approach to the Wisdom Literature of the Old Testament* (Grand Rapids: Eerdmans, 1996), pp. 50–119.
[7] Paul boasts in hardships and delights in difficulties in a number of his letters to the early churches. See Rom 5.3–4; 2 Cor 4.10–11; Phil 1.29–30.
[8] Matt 26.39 NRSV.
[9] In the Old Testament, Israel's obedience to the Law is a grateful expression of loyalty that rests squarely upon their (undeserved) deliverance from Egypt. In fact, the Ten Commandments in Exodus 20.3–17 begin with this premise: 'I am the LORD your God, who brought you out of the land of Egypt, out of the house of slavery' (Exod 20.2 NRSV). The Old Testament justice system is thus an expression of God's grace.

By the same token, the New Testament proclaims that on the cross Jesus paid the penalty for the sin of the world. If God were only a

God of grace, he could simply have said, 'I forgive all of humanity's sin and no longer hold any of it against them', and left it at that. But the *necessity* of the cross and Jesus' suffering indicates that guilt and sin could not simply be cancelled out and forgotten. Jesus satisfied God's requirement for justice. It is overly simplistic (and theologically inaccurate) to say that the OT promotes justice and the NT promotes grace.

[10] The parable of the lost sons in Luke 15 makes this point with penetrating insight. I say lost *sons* because both the runaway son and the stay-at-home son misunderstand their father's love. Both think that they must earn their father's gifts and approval. See Lk 15.19,29.

[11] On the brokenness of the world or the messiness of life, see ch. 2, n. 13 (on p. 95).

[12] Isa 25.9 NKJV.

www.ingramcontent.com/pod-product-compliance
Lightning Source LLC
Chambersburg PA
CBHW071221160426
43196CB00012B/2370